QUALITY DEPENDS ON *YOU*

7 SIMPLE THINGS YOU CAN DO FOR YOUR COMPANY AND YOUR CAREER

WRITER: DAVID DEE

ILLUSTRATOR:
DAVE CALVER

DARTNELL is a publisher serving the world of business with book manuals, newsletters and bulletins, and training materials for executives, managers, supervisors, salespeople, financial officials, personnel executives, and office employees. Dartnell also produces management and sales training videos and audiocassettes, publishes many useful business forms, and many of its materials and films are available in languages other than English. Dartnell, established in 1917, serves the world's business community. For details, catalogs, and product information, write:

THE DARTNELL CORPORATION
4660 N. Ravenswood Ave.
Chicago, IL 60640-4595, U.S.A.
or phone (800) 621-5463 in U.S. and Canada

This publication is designed to provide accurate and authoritative information in regard to the subject matter covered. It is sold with the understanding that the publisher is not engaged in rendering legal, accounting, or other professional service. If legal advice or other expert assistance is required, the services of a competent professional person should be sought.

From a Declaration of Principles jointly adopted by a Committee of the American Bar Association and a Committee of Publishers.

Copyright 1996 in the United States, Canada, and Britain by
THE DARTNELL CORPORATION
Library of Congress Catalog Card Number: 96-083847
ISBN 0-85013-251-7

Printed in the United States of America by
The Dartnell Press, Chicago, IL 60640-4595

CONTENTS   PAGE

CHAPTER 9: CREATING QUALITY
FRONTLINE CUSTOMER SERVICE 221

INTRODUCTION

"Quality Depends on *You*" is unlike any other book you've read. In the past, all the literature about quality in the workplace has focused on product quality and management of quality companies. The result? A wealth of material focusing on *processes,* such as eliminating manufacturing defects and refining quality methods and procedures.

"Quality Depends on *You*" takes quality awareness to a new frontier: personal quality. We developed this book because far too little attention has been paid to improving the quality of the *people* whose efforts are crucial for any quality initiative to succeed. After all, where quality is concerned, it is the individual who makes all the difference. If everyone in your company or organization did their best every day to produce quality work, all other components of quality would fall into place.

In "Quality Depends on *You,*" we show you how to create and implement a personal quality plan of action, which will immediately begin to improve your productivity and strengthen the quality of your work. The result? Greater job satisfaction.

"Quality Depends on *You*" also is a career-builder. This book isn't simply about how to do your current job better. It's about seeing your role as a quality provider from a new perspective. It's about choosing quality in everything you do.

You don't leave your new personal quality outlook on your desk when you go home at night: It's ingrained in all you do. For this reason, we're sure that the new way of thinking you'll learn from utilizing the tips and techniques in this book will help you well beyond your current position. Your new quality outlook will strengthen your chances for promotion and will make you more desirable in the job market.

The heart of this book's plan is a list of *The 7 Simple Things You Can Do for Your Company and Your Career.* To devise this list, we studied several leading quality improvement programs to find the elements that make them succeed. We narrowed these key points down to seven. In the first seven chapters of this book, we show you how to transform these simple ideas into specific actions that can improve your personal quality right now:

1. Make Continuous Improvement Your Personal Motto

2. Be a *Super* Supplier to *Your* Customers

3. Zero In on Zero Defects

4. Reengineer Your Thinking

5. Believe in Your Own Quality

6. Sign Your Work

7. Benchmark the Best.

Each action step is illustrated with real examples and practical, how-to tips on making the "simple thing" relevant to everything you do. You'll learn how to set high personal standards for yourself as well as how to demand and receive high levels of quality from others. Whether you work in manufacturing or in an office, and whether you have daily customer contact or no customer contact at all, you'll gain a new perspective on quality and the critical role you play in producing quality work every day.

Chapters 8, 9, and 10 are jam-packed with specific quality improvement tips aimed specifically for supervisors, customer service reps, administrative assistants, and other office support staff.

All chapters include tips from experts, anecdotes, case studies, motivational quotes, quizzes, and a quick overview, *Your Quality Take-Away*. "Quality Depends on *You*" consists of material from Dartnell's popular *Quality 1st* office bulletin as well as new material and new sources.

If you're like most frontline workers, you've found that for far too long, the concept of quality has been elusive. There has been a lot of talk about what quality is, but far too little understanding of what each individual can do to achieve it. We hope you'll find that "Quality Depends on *You*" finally brings quality to the personal level — where it's always belonged.

— The Editors

PART I

THE 7 SIMPLE
THINGS YOU CAN DO

CHAPTER ONE

MAKE CONTINUOUS IMPROVEMENT YOUR PERSONAL MOTTO

"The quality of a person's life is in direct proportion to their commitment to excellence, regardless of their chosen field of endeavor."
— VINCE LOMBARDI (1913–1970),
AMERICAN PROFESSIONAL FOOTBALL COACH

INTRODUCTION

The central, unifying concept of every quality approach is that everything an organization does is part of a continuous improvement process. In industry, continuous improvement means that no process, product, or service ever attains perfection. It is only through deliberate, ongoing, positive changes that an organization can keep up with the expectations of its customers and with the quality of its competitors.

Although most of us don't think of it in the same terms, we all adapt the concept of continuous improvement to some degree to our own lives. We go on diets to lose weight and improve our health; we take courses to remain competitive in the job market; and we look for ways to do our jobs better so we can advance in our careers. Making continuous improvement a personal motto means having a personal commitment to making gradual positive changes that will improve your job performance and bring you closer to attaining your career goals. Committing to a path of continuous personal improvement should be the first step you take toward your goal of enhancing your personal quality.

There is no formula for personal improvement that applies to everyone. Each of us has our own particular strengths and weaknesses. For continuous improvement to be effective, it's important for us to know which areas of our personal and professional lives need improvement, and how much.

One of the most effective ways to uncover our own strengths and weaknesses is through the use of a personal checklist. Harry Roberts, professor emeritus of statistics and quality management at the University of Chicago Graduate School of Business, developed the concept of creating checklists to measure personal quality. He explains the process in detail in *Quality Is Personal* (The Free Press), which he coauthored with Bernard F. Sergesketter, vice president of the central region of AT&T in Chicago.

A personal quality checklist lets employees keep track of desirable personal job-performance traits and failures. The checklist is not only useful for training about quality but has an astonishing potential for quickly improving general work effectiveness and for improving quality in everyday life.

Creating and using this type of checklist is not difficult. In fact, Roberts says that the simplicity of the personal quality checklist often creates skepticism about its potential benefits and that the only way to convince yourself of its usefulness is to try it.

The checklist is started by listing the processes you personally use to do your work. "Almost everyone uses meetings, telephone calls, and correspondence in one way or another," explain the authors. "Also, it's important for everyone to make a good appearance and to stay healthy." With that in mind co-author Sergesketter developed his own checklist, which included work-related items such as being on time for meetings; answering the phone in two rings or less; returning calls the same day or next day; responding to letters within five business days; and keeping his desk clean. It also included personal items such as "keep weight below 190 pounds" and "exercise at least three times per week."

"Once you decide what constitutes good personal quality, simply mark down failures or defects as they occur and try to prevent them in the future," says Roberts. For example, if a day passed in which Sergesketter did not return a phone call on the same or next business day, he recorded a defect in that area for that day.

Monitor your defects every day and every week. "You cannot reduce the number of defects in your processes if you don't count them," explain the authors. "When defects occur regularly in one category, sit down and figure out how you can improve in that category."

Sergesketter, for example, was surprised by the defects he was recording in one particular area. "The extent to which I was not returning calls on the same or next day was high — this was a surprise to me." Roberts reports that upon implementing the checklist, Sergesketter found a substantial drop in the number of defects and an improvement in his job performance. He then challenged his associates to make a list of five things that would help them meet their personal and business needs and to count defects with a goal of 68 percent annual improvement. The challenge paid off: Meetings now start on time, end on time, and are more businesslike. And Sergesketter has found an extra hour a day because of the checklist approach.

The checklist will provide insights into areas where you can improve. In this chapter, we look at a number of other ways to make continuous improvement a motivating force in both your work and your personal life.

Break Away from the 'Been There, Done That' Mold

Although you're very good at what you do, you're beginning to feel a little bored at your job. You like what you're doing and don't want to leave, but is there any other way to break free from the same old routine?

Take these positive steps to make your current position more exciting, and pull yourself out of your rut:

- **Learn a new job skill.** Mastering a new computer software program or developing expertise in a particular area can do wonders for your outlook. Broaden your horizons by acquiring knowledge.

- **Expand your network.** Establishing productive relationships with people both inside and outside your organization can give your career new life. Learn what you can from others, and give of your own experience as well.

- **Set goals for yourself.** Give yourself something to work for, and reward yourself when you achieve it. If you can't think of any goals, then it's your mind that's stuck in a rut — not your job.

- **Ask for more responsibility.** Shake up your routine by throwing some new duties into the mix. You'll show that you're a team player and earn allies by helping your peers.

There's more than one way to put some variety into your work life. Make sure that you look at all of your options — and the consequences of each — before deciding how to go about recharging your career.

BECOME A 'VALUE-ADDED' TEAM MEMBER

It's easy to become so immersed in getting your job done that you lose sight of the qualities that make you an asset to your organization. To assess your "current value," consider the qualities employers look for when they're hiring, suggests Roslyn Kunin, president of Roslyn Kunin & Associates, a management consulting firm in Vancouver, British Columbia. A survey by the Business Council of British Columbia reveals nine such qualities. Honing these work attributes, Kunin says, can make you an even greater asset to your organization.

1. Highly developed communication skills. "If you're a good communicator, you're also a good listener," Kunin notes. You can speak clearly using proper grammar. You're skilled with written words as well and are able to write a business letter or report that clearly conveys what you want to say and reflects the quality of your company and its products.

2. Analytical ability. "This is your ability to recognize a problem, take that problem apart, and then find and apply a solution," says Kunin.

3. High standards. Set high standards for yourself for performance, accuracy, and commitment to your organization. "Then meet or even surpass those standards," advises Kunin.

4. Honesty and reliability. Trustworthy employees are highly valued. Reliability is also important, which means showing up for work on time, working the hours expected of you and a little extra, if needed.

5. Flexibility and adaptability. "In our fast-paced world, machines, jobs, and products come, go, and metamorphose with amazing speed," Kunin observes. "All of us must be willing and able to learn and change in order to fit into the current and future job market."

6. Team spirit. Employees who are supportive, friendly, cooperative, and helpful are highly prized, Kunin emphasizes.

They know how to get along with their bosses, peers, and others — both inside and outside the organization.

7. Positive attitudes. "Attitudes can be measured by what you say about your work, your company, or your boss when you think no one important is listening," Kunin points out. The way we convey our personal attitudes is really a matter of habit, she notes. So, it's within our power to change negativity and get into the habit of displaying positive attitudes.

8. Productivity. When assessing your own level of productivity Kunin advises, "Bear in mind that you were originally hired because you were expected to add value to the organization." What you actually accomplish really does count.

9. Intelligence. Kunin notes that machines have replaced people in jobs where brains aren't needed. "This means that, in the job you do today, you really need to bring your brain to work!"

'VISIONEERING' BRINGS QUALITY DREAM TO LIFE

Quality isn't the child of total quality management or quality circles. It's born in your mind — and in the minds of your teammates. For that reason, having a vision is an important part of the quality relationship.

"Since we all ultimately become what we think, say, and do, it's critical to understand the meaning of visioneering," explains Joe Batten, author of *Building a Total Quality Culture* (Crisp Publications).

"A *vision* is the situation we see in our minds. We visualize the macro [large-scale] results we want to achieve. A *mission* is a generally targeted and focused statement of intended macro results. It's the basis for more specific goals. And, a *dream* is a deeply felt and yearned for hope of the possible."

From these, Batten says, a quality-oriented philosophy evolves. It's a body of beliefs that generates the birth of the dream, the stimulation of the vision, and the formation of the mission. In other words, it's the driving force behind your team's quality efforts.

To be a leading member of your quality team, you must recognize your team's vision and help everyone move toward that ideal. "We must pull our team members toward macro commitments that are larger than ourselves," says Batten.

Without a vision, the quality consultant points out, we have no clear focus. The absence of a dream leaves us with no renewal of hope. Worst of all, our work, and even our lives, have no real meaning when we're devoid of a philosophy. "Leading, pulling, stretching, reaching, and striving upward and onward are the marks of the visioneer," Batten says.

Here are some of the beliefs that contribute to a visioneering quality culture:

- Change is the world's only constant. While losers seek shelter in static stability, winners thrive on the vitality of new challenges.

- Visioneers ask, listen, and hear. They don't tell, command, or coerce. To have a vision is to act as a guide — not a commander.

Tough-minded visioneers possess these attributes: confidence, self-respect, courage, commitment, integrity, moral values, resilience, tenacity, sensitivity to change, and a belief in something or someone greater than themselves.

- Enlightened visioneers realize that human effort can and must be concentrated and focused like a laser beam.

- Peak performers are motivated by an all-consuming commitment to a transcendent vision, dream, or mission.

- The best organizations and people are driven by values. They don't seek bigger profits by compromising quality.

Consider these points as you nurture the vision in your mind into a reality for your quality team.

IDEA IN ACTION

TEAMS FUEL CONTINUOUS IMPROVEMENT EFFORTS

Just as continuous improvement is necessary for success in today's business environment, so are effective teams necessary for the process of continuous improvement to succeed.

Fisher-Rosemount, a Chanhassen, Minnesota-based manufacturer of pressure transmitters, depends on the ideas and actions of cross-functional teams to keep quality improving. The cross-functional aspect is important because each team possesses the knowledge and capabilities to solve any problem. "You want teams to be organized in a way that they can solve any problem without having to go to any outside resources," says Edward Monser, vice president of pressure operations for Fisher-Rosemount.

Fisher-Rosemount offers a two-part foundation for continuous improvement: 1. have an effective early warning system; and 2. take quick corrective action. These goals are instrumental because delays in the identification or solution of a problem mean lost time and money. "If you had to shut your factory down whenever there was a problem, how fast would you want to solve it?" Monser speculates.

To meet these goals, Fisher-Rosemount has set up several teams that include members from all areas of the organization. Among these teams are the PIT (process improvement team) crews, which bring together six to 12 instrument builders, manufacturing engineers and technicians, and designers to address reduction problems.

PIT crews are called into action when an instrument builder flips on the red light at his or her station at the first indication of a problem as part of the early warning system. The teams then identify the problem and devise an immediate solution. Instrument builders are especially helpful in this action, since they are cross-trained to fully understand each part of the production process.

But the teams aren't only reactive; they receive input that allows them to take proactive steps as well. For example, team members are given figures that track scrap and costs, which allow them to see where the problem areas are and to come up with ideas to fix them.

The combination of proactive and reactive team ideas has been invaluable to Fisher-Rosemount. On one product model alone, the company implemented 216 team suggestions that cut the cost of scrap material by 43 percent, improved "out-of-box" quality by 80 percent, halved order lead times from 12 weeks to six weeks, and cut cycle time by 75 percent.

These and similar developments initiated by team members enable Fisher-Rosemount to deliver on its promise of continuous improvement — a necessity for keeping customers. "We have to show customers that we're improving faster than our competition," Monser says. Customers are only going to buy your product or service if it will give them an advantage over their competition, he adds. "That's what keeps them competitive."

YES, *YOU* CAN LEAD THE WAY

There aren't enough jobs at the top for everyone, but aren't there *leaders* at every level in every organization? "Yes," says Geoffrey M. Bellman, "you can lead when you are not in a position of authority. Yes, you can lead when everyone you are working with outranks you. Yes, you can lead when you are new to an organization or a situation."

Leadership on a small scale may be as simple as redesigning a work process, he explains in *Getting Things Done When You're Not in Charge* (Berrett-Koehler). "Leadership is based upon a belief in yourself, and in the people you work with, in your job, in the future, and in the ability to achieve something more."

In today's economic climate, leading may well mean finding new ways to do more with less. Bellman suggests the following ways in which you can help your team "tighten its belt" and to display your ability to be a leader at the same time:

- Don't wait until the pressure is on to trim waste. Says Bellman: "Keep it trim all the time. We must pay attention to what we need to do and what size we need to be to do it, and then make sure that we are that size now."

- Find more effective ways of doing what you are already doing. Ask yourself: "If you weren't doing it this way, how would you do it?" If you come up with more efficient ways, suggest them to your team.

- Always be on the lookout for ways to save money. If you can reduce downtime, for example, do it, and make sure your supervisors know it.

"Leading is not primarily the sweeping, revolutionary action that is likely to put us on the cover of *Business Week*," says Bellman. "I see all of us as having the possibility of leading, especially on a small scale."

How Can You Add Value to the Bottom Line?

All companies that want to survive must pay attention to the bottom line. So when teams can show a positive effect on productivity and, thus, profitability, they shine in the company's eyes. The secret is to show your employer how you can bring extra value to the organization. Dale Winston, president of Battalia Winston International, a search firm based in New York City, has 10 tips:

1. Aside from team goals, set personal objectives.

2. As situations change within your workplace, go after new targets.

3. Meet your objectives.

4. Using what you've already achieved as a benchmark, work hard for advancement.

5. Build strong ties both within and outside your team. Support one another, and praise your teammates to higher-ups.

6. Follow your company's progress by reading the business pages and listening.

7. Develop a keen knowledge of what your company and industry are all about.

8. Volunteer for extra tasks, broaden your talents, and learn to train yourself.

9. Go to company picnics and other outings. Be a joiner and a booster.

10. Ask for and give advice whenever you or a coworker need it.

"Complacency has no part in today's workplace," Winston declares. "If you want to advance, increase your value. Those who rest on their laurels won't go far."

A FIELD DAY OF VALUES

Marshall Field, the pioneering Chicago department store magnate, once indicated the following reminders that can be helpful in obtaining a sound sense of values. They offer an excellent roadmap today to guide us in our own personal quality goals at home and at work:

1. The value of time.

2. The success of perseverance.

3. The pleasure of working.

4. The dignity of simplicity.

5. The worth of character.

6. The power of kindness.

7. The influence of example.

8. The obligation of duty.

9. The wisdom of economy.

10. The virtue of patience.

11. The improvement of talent.

AVOID THIS TRAP

Don't let your goal of continuous personal improvement force you into the "perfectionist trap." Perfectionists feel they must be flawless in everything they do. At work, they can't move on to other tasks until they feel the project they are working on is as perfect as can be. However, in striving for everything to be perfect, perfectionists may be setting a standard that is impossible to achieve. They may be sabotaging their own careers by becoming so blinded by the details of a project that they forget the big picture.

The costs of perfectionism can be more than psychological. Perfectionists may be actually putting themselves in physical peril. A new study by Lorraine and J. Clayton Lafferty — clinical psychologists in Plymouth, Michigan — links perfectionism to coronary problems, ulcers, and migraines. In a *Chicago Tribune* interview, Lorraine Lafferty, manager of Human Synergistics International, a consulting firm, said, "Perfectionists are never satisfied with their performance. They have difficulty getting closure on anything because they're so focused on making sure it's perfect. Their superiors and colleagues may end up doubting their competence."

Here are a few steps you can take to escape the perfectionist trap:

1. Set priorities. "If you're sending out a letter to the corporate board of directors, it must be letter-perfect. But if you're sending out a memo to announce a staff meeting, it doesn't have to be perfect," says Connie Glaser, coauthor of *Swim with the Dolphins: How Women Can Succeed in Corporate America on Their Own Terms* (Warner Books). "I'm not advocating mediocrity. What I am advocating is that you become more selective about setting priorities. You shouldn't labor over every single aspect of your job."

2. Change your self-talk. Do you find yourself constantly thinking, "I should have …"? Try to stop yourself the next time you think that. Instead, get in the habit of congratulating yourself for doing a good job.

3. Focus on the process. Perfectionists tend to focus on the end result. Instead, look at the path you took to get where you are. Start appreciating the journey and patting yourself on the back for the decisions you've made, the deadlines you've met, and the lessons you've learned along the way.

4. Accept your mistakes. Errors are part of life. Everyone makes them; however, by doing high-priority tasks well and getting work out to the right people, your occasional mistakes will be overlooked. Learn to live with the mistakes you make and then move on.

MONITOR YOUR PRODUCTIVITY TO GAUGE YOUR IMPROVEMENT

Most people need some sort of yardstick by which to measure their personal performance. For some, it's a paycheck; for others, it's a "Well done!" from a colleague or boss. Most of us, however, measure our effectiveness by how productive we are. In most companies, productivity is one of the driving forces of workplace performance.

Virtually anyone who receives a performance evaluation knows that productivity enters into the picture. After all, it's one thing that supervisors notice and consider. But most conscientious workers also use their personal productivity as a benchmark for their individual successes.

Richard Ott, consultant and author of *Unleashing Productivity!* (Irwin), claims that all of us have untapped resources of productivity. "To be productive," he says, "you must take action — consistently." Ott also points out the huge gulf between "busywork" and real action (which produces results). How can you boost your personal productivity?

- **Talk to people.** Few of us work alone. Our productivity generally requires the cooperation and assistance of coworkers, the recognition of supervisors, and information from many sources. Talking to people provides the input we need to do our jobs effectively.

- **Commit.** Cautious or uncertain people accomplish relatively little. To be productive, says Ott, you must obligate yourself to a task. You must say, "I will do it!" and mean it.

- **Engage in physical movement.** Sure, many jobs don't require great physical activity, but Ott believes that some kind of movement is crucial to productivity. One can't take action, he says, without making a move, be it opening a book, typing a report, or loading a truck.

- **Determine how much information is sufficient.** Because there's no such thing as total certainty, the productive person must gather enough information to make a decision — then act. Stalling to get more information is inaction.

- **Act in the face of judgment.** Those who worry about what others may think of their actions usually stop being productive — they're too afraid to make a move. If you know when to act, eventually you'll realize that others aren't scrutinizing you as closely as you think.

- **Don't be discouraged by others.** Do coworkers always tell you that your plans won't work? For some reason, people find it easier to squash new ideas than to give them a try. Don't be dismayed by naysayers who are too afraid to take a risk themselves.

- **Don't get trapped by blame.** Blaming others for a failure or mistake is the essence of nonproductivity. Instead, sidestep blame, and keep the action alive. When others stand idle and blame each other, step forward and offer a plan of action.

- **Accept risk.** Worthwhile action involves risk. You might be risking time, money, resources, or credibility. Often, people tend to exaggerate risk and focus on the worst that can happen.

Mastering these suggestions not only can help you work smarter, but produce more. No doubt, you'll soon discover that your productivity does indeed measure up — and that's a sure sign that you're steadily improving your performance.

TAKE A DEEP BREATH ... NOW ASK FOR A PERFORMANCE CHECKUP

Do you honestly know what the higher-ups think of your job performance? You're smart to find out. Rather than waiting for your annual performance appraisal, *ask* your boss for a job review before the scheduled time rolls around.

Specifically, ask for ways you can improve your own performance. Don't be afraid to ask questions when you don't understand a particular comment or criticism. Also, ask the boss to focus on the future. Assuming that you follow recommendations, where could you be in a year or two? What skills do you need to get there?

Asking for feedback — rather than waiting for it — shows that you want to contribute your best and move up the career ladder.

MAKE WAY FOR 'MULTIRATER' FEEDBACK

If your team and its environment are typical, feedback for performance appraisals and development probably comes from a limited number of sources: your boss or manager, your team leader, and perhaps your fellow teammates. A new system called "multirater" feedback (MRF) could prove to change that. Previously used primarily by upper-level managers who evaluated their own efforts through outside consulting firms, MRF first was used by work teams in the early 1990s.

MRF is a process based on necessary job skills. Teammates can use it both for personal development and team performance appraisals.

MRF also provides feedback from numerous sources, which may include your boss or manager, your team leader, your supervisor, your teammates, the internal customers with whom you work most closely, and people from outside your team whom you see frequently. "You also can rate yourself," notes Susan H. Gebelein, senior vice president of Personnel Decisions International (PDI) in Minneapolis.

Gebelein believes the principal advantage of MRF is that you can look at your skills from a much broader perspective. "You get feedback from your peers and those both above and below your work level. MRF is sometimes called '360 degree' feedback because it can involve anyone in the company circle," she notes. The result is a more complete and, thus, helpful skill analysis.

MRF is most effective in large and midsize organizations, Gebelein says. In a small workplace, a less formal system can accomplish the same results. Seventy-five percent of all the Fortune 500 companies, she estimates, are currently using some form of MRF. PDI is working with half of that elite group to integrate the process into their training programs.

The anonymity associated with the use of MRF contributes to its success as an evaluation tool. When people are just one part of an evaluation tool, they are more likely to be honest and objective than they would be with single-person judgments. If MRF is used for performance appraisals, the results are shared only with your boss or manager. Then it becomes part of your performance file. In other words, using MRF doesn't mean enduring "multi-exposure."

MRF has at least equal value as a developmental or performance-management device. Sprint, Amoco, AT&T, and Ford Motor Company are among the PDI clients that are implementing the plan.

In most companies, Gebelein says, employees aren't required to disclose their MRF results for developmental purposes. Nevertheless, PDI has found that between 50 percent and 75 percent of those involved in the program reveal results on a voluntary basis. They want coaching because they see it as an avenue to advancement. Therefore, they are willing to undergo future scrutiny.

MRF won't work unless everyone cooperates and contributes. If this evaluation tool sounds like something your team could benefit from, take the initiative and talk to management about a trial. An evaluation should be a real learning experience. There's great wisdom within your company circle, and it can enable you to do a better job for your team ... and yourself.

WANTED: SUGGESTIONS!

If your company or work team doesn't already have a suggestion system, you can help to get one started. Ideas from employees save companies money, increase worker morale, and often earn incentives. They can be an important element of a company's continuous improvement efforts. And they can work at the department as well as company-wide level.

The pioneer employee suggestion program was developed in 1898 by Eastman Kodak Company. Today, more than 900 organizations are members of the nonprofit National Association of Suggestion Systems (NASS). Outside NASS, many other employee suggestion plans are in operation. The total in the United States, NASS estimates, is probably more than 6,000. Thanks to worker creativity, companies with suggestion programs save more than $2 billion a year.

For a suggestion system to succeed, designated employees should work with top management. NASS offers this blueprint for success:

- Recruit the dedicated support of management.

- Working with company leaders, map the objectives of the program long before it's implemented.

- Ask your supervisor to help launch the flow of ideas.

- If company officials are receptive, set up an awards program. Many organizations give plaques, dinners at fine restaurants, or cash as incentives to employees whose suggestions are put into effect.

- Explain to your coworkers how the program will function. And, ask the editor of your company's employee publication to promote the effort.

- With management, try to organize a plan under which all suggestions — not just the winners — are acknowledged.

As one example of a successful U.S. effort, Cincinnati Bell Telephone started its program in 1984. The company has received more than 1,800 suggestions from its 900 employees. Robert Grubbs, coordinator of the plan, says that winning ideas have covered everything from technical refinements to speedier methods of customer billing. Says Grubbs: "Our goal is to have everyone in the company participate. We value our employees' suggestions."

ALL SUGGESTION SYSTEMS ARE NOT ALIKE!

Motto No. 1: "We want every suggestion, regardless of its monetary value!"

Motto No. 2: "Our system is designated to generate problems that need to be addressed!"

Two companies can take different approaches to employee involvement, as the mottoes above indicate. But the goal is the same — getting great ideas from employees. Suggestion programs offer employees an outlet for their analytical and creative abilities while providing the organizations they work for with cost-cutting, quality-boosting ideas. The benefits to both parties are great, as RLI Insurance and Reflexite Corporation — the companies whose suggestion mottoes are listed above — can attest.

RLI Insurance of Peoria, Illinois, has a four-year-old on-line employee suggestion system designed to highlight the value of employee ideas (Motto No. 1). "We designed our own system for getting employee suggestions," reports Kim Breese, recognition coordinator for RLI. "None of them met our needs. We found that too many were complex and required employees to fill out a lot of forms. That slows down the number of responses. We wanted creative suggestions coming in fast and easily."

And they got them. The first year of the program, 300 suggestions were submitted through the company's electronic mail system. That number rose to more than 900 — 650 of which were accepted — the next year.

"Every suggestion is acknowledged with a $2 thank you note," says Breese. Each one is then routed to the first-line employee in the company who can best judge what, if any, action should be taken. Employees whose suggestions are accepted are eligible for a $50 or $100 prize. Extra effort produces extra recognition. Five accepted suggestions or one that produces a savings of at least $5,000 earns membership on the company's "all-star" team.

Reflexite Corporation of Avon, Connecticut, takes a different, but equally effective, approach to recruiting suggestions. An employee-owned maker of retroflective materials, such as highway safety cones, Reflexite uses EARS — Employee Assistance Request System — to solicit employee ideas. The program was designed to encourage employees to raise questions about how to improve the total quality of the company's products. Employees submit problems that make their jobs difficult. Every problem is then logged into the system, no matter how simple or complex.

"Then it is assigned to an action leader to lead the process for solving the problem," notes David Edgar, Reflexite's vice president of human resources. Employees are given up to eight hours and $500 to devise a solution. Since the company is employee-owned, there are no cash awards, but everyone benefits from improved productivity. For example, one problem raised was hazardous waste disposal. The employees addressing the issue designed a system for disposal that saves the company between $30,000 and $40,000 annually. "This system increases employee ownership and commitment to problem solving. The challenge of solving the problems is something that taps creativity and produces solutions we find so exciting," says Edgar.

The suggestion systems of both RLI Insurance and Reflexite both rely on employee concern and involvement. The differences in their systems show that the issue can be addressed from many angles.

QUICK TIPS

- **Strengthen those communication skills.** To improve your chances for workplace success, improve your writing skills. With the surge in office e-mail and Internet services, employees are actually writing more today than a few years ago, reports *The Wall Street Journal*. People who know you only by your computer persona will judge your professionalism and skill based on how well you communicate in writing.

- **Set a deadline for making decisions.** Tough decision to make? Tell yourself, "I will decide how to address this issue in the next 15 minutes." Then start thinking, and stick to your deadline.

- **Accept criticism.** To get honest feedback from peers and supervisors, you need to be prepared to accept it. Don't ask for someone's opinion and then discount it or get angry if you don't like it. Instead, separate yourself from the criticism by focusing on the behavior being addressed.

- **Make quality a way of life.** Quality concepts don't stop when you walk out the door at the end of the workday. Many people who are involved in quality initiatives on the job find that those ideas can be applied to family and personal issues as well. Team building can be used to get rival siblings to cooperate. Cycle-time procedures can help you get more done in less time, so you can focus on leisure activities. So, take home with you what you learn at work.

- **Prepare for the future.** Specific work talents will be needed in tomorrow's workplace, says Carolyn Woo, director of the graduate program at Purdue University's Krannert School of Management. They include advanced analytical capability, project-management skills, and a sense of accountability and stewardship, says Woo. Make sure your continuous improvement efforts specifically include strengthening your abilities in those areas.

- **Assess yourself.** If you were given a performance appraisal tomorrow, could you tell your boss everything you have accomplished during the past six to 12 months? Each week, list your achievements and keep a running log of them. Then, when your boss asks what you've done lately, you'll be able to provide accurate information quickly and easily.

DRAFT YOUR 'PERSONAL PERFORMANCE' CONTRACT

"Everyone in our company is going to have to sign a 'personal performance' contract. I know this involves setting individual goals for work performance, but I don't know much else about it. What do I need to know?"

— B.N.D., Ottawa, Ontario

"A personal performance contract (PPC) is a written agreement between an employee and his or her manager that records accomplishments to be achieved within a specific time period," according to Roger Fritz in *Personal Performance Contracts* (Crisp Publications). The process involves a careful job analysis, preparation of a list of objectives, an action plan, a time-and-cost schedule, a self-development program, and regular reviews of progress.

The following quiz will help you better understand PPCs. Write True or False after each statement.

1. A PPC should address work details you might forget. _____

2. The best PPC covers goals that are easily accomplished. _____

3. The first step in preparing a PPC is to set objectives. _____

4. Accountability is determining who will do what by when. _____

5. Your PPC should concentrate on high-priority tasks. _____

6. A PPC should be written from the employee's point of view. _____

7. The key to job success is planned, sustained effort. _____

8. When you're preparing your PPC, you should discuss your strengths and weaknesses with your boss. _____

9. An individual PPC need not necessarily relate to company goals. _____

10. It's wise to use the PPC to measure every aspect of
your job.   _____

YOUR PPC SAVVY: Statements 4, 5, 7, and 8 are True. Here's why the others are False: (1) a PPC should focus on your basic responsibilities; (2) the best results are achieved through extra effort; (3) objectives can be meaningless without an analysis of your needs; (6) you and your boss must both contribute to the final contract; (9) any PPC should directly relate to your employer's priorities; (10) measurement should zero in on key result areas. Don't be afraid to ask questions and make suggestions during the creation of your contract. It has as much to do with you as it does with your company.

YOUR QUALITY TAKE-AWAY

The First Simple Thing You Can Do for
Your Company and Your Career:

Make Continuous Improvement
Your Personal Motto

In manufacturing, continuous improvement means that no action or procedure is perfect, and that it is only through small, incremental ongoing positive changes that organizations can remain competitive. In organizations, suggestion programs help departments and teams continuously improve their methods and processes. Some companies utilize cross-functional teams to uncover new ways to improve processes and procedures. Adapting that concept to the personal quality level will keep you competent and competitive on the job and throughout your career.

What *You* Can Do

- Seek performance appraisals from your boss and from coworkers.

- Maintain a personal checklist to track professional and personal strengths and weaknesses.

- Act like a leader — even if you don't have a position of authority — and be a value-added team member.

- Utilize techniques like "visioneering," which can help you focus on personal and team goals. Cultivate values. Strengthen communication and time management skills.

Continuous improvement begins with you. High levels of personal quality contribute to high levels of team, department, and organizational improvement. Get the momentum going!

CHAPTER TWO

BE A <u>SUPER</u> SUPPLIER TO YOUR 'CUSTOMERS'

"Would you do business with you?"
— LINDA SILVERMAN GOLDZIMER,
AUTHOR OF *I'M FIRST: YOUR CUSTOMER'S MESSAGE TO YOU*
(RAWSON ASSOCIATES)

INTRODUCTION

In traditional management, all the attention is focused on the organization's external customer — the end users of the organization's products or services. When companies embrace a quality program, they widen their view of customers and begin paying closer attention to a second, equally important customer: the internal customer.

In most organizations, different departments and their employees are, literally, each other's customers. The ultimate aim of a company is to satisfy its customers. Only when departments can satisfy the needs of others internally can the organization satisfy the external customer. For example, by understanding your particular organization, its people, and all of its services, you will know who to contact if a customer, business associate, or you need something that is handled by another department.

Try this: On paper, begin a chart with three headings: Department (for listing all your company's departments); Product (what those departments are responsible for); and Contacts (who in that area you can call for help). Keep this list on hand. Not only will you have a better understanding of where your job fits into the big picture, but you'll also be able to identify how you can help your coworkers. Here are other ways to be a super supplier to your internal customers:

- **Respond to their requests.** When a coworker calls, get back to him or her quickly. Another employee may need your expertise to serve a client. You'll encourage coworkers to return your calls quickly if that's the treatment they get from you.

- **Be a team player.** If you find a handy tip for performing a task, let others know about it. Share information about new products and services.

- **Lend a helping hand.** Is that phone at the next desk ringing? Answer it. Does a coworker need files you can locate? Retrieve them. Is a colleague trying to serve three customers simultaneously while two more wait? Help out.

- **Communicate.** Don't depend on managers to relay all the information you need. Take it upon yourself to keep the flow of communications going between work areas and departments. Get to know each other and understand each other's needs. Isn't that what makes customer service succeed?

How else can you provide quality service to *all* your customers? The following ideas will point the way.

'OUT OF SIGHT' SHOULDN'T MEAN 'OUT OF MIND'

Your Midwest salesperson needs updates on product availability and shipping schedules for potential customers. The problem is that she calls late in the day, just minutes before the office staff in the East is getting ready to leave for the day. Reps are letting the line go unanswered so they can leave on time.

The modern business often has a number of offices spread out across a country or even across continents. When you work with people who are removed from your immediate area, it's easy to forget that you all work for the same organization and share the same goals. But this long-distance operation doesn't dismiss the need for teamwork. In fact, it makes it even more important.

To achieve peak performance, teammates on all levels and at all locations must cooperate. Your support of coworkers who are in the field, at another office, or in another department is key to your ultimate success. If reps are ignoring calls from the Midwest sales rep because she calls late in the day, that salesperson is working at a disadvantage — and so is the company. A competitor is able to provide potential customers with quick answers to questions, while our salesperson must wait to obtain crucial data that may not come for days. A lack of cooperation works against potential sales and profits. All callers to the office are entitled to be welcomed up until closing time. Conversely, the sales rep shouldn't expect lengthy reports when coworkers are leaving for the day.

Discuss the time problem with the salesperson. She may not be thinking about the time zone difference and may have no idea she is causing an inconvenience. Remember, when you serve her, you are indirectly serving your outside customers as well.

ACROSS TOWN OR ACROSS THE HALL?
THEY'RE BOTH YOUR CUSTOMERS

To his coworkers, Carlos seemed confused about who he had on the phone. A caller from another department in the main building was asking Carlos to send over a skid of paper that was stored in the warehouse. "Mr. Barnes, our truck leaves in 25 minutes," Carlos told the caller. "So, I'll have the paper there by 3 p.m. Is that acceptable? Great. Thanks for calling."

As soon as Carlos hung up the phone, his coworkers in the warehouse began to tease him. "Carlos, that was Ben. You play basketball with him every Wednesday night. What's this 'Mr. Barnes' business?" Carlos was not about to be intimidated. "He's Ben on the court. Right now he's my customer."

Carlos realized that his organization has two customers: those who purchase the product or service his company produces — the outside customers — and the other employees of the organization — the inside customers. "My job is to serve my customers in the building, so they can serve the customers who bring in money," Carlos explains. "If we both don't do our part, that outside customer is going to do his business somewhere else."

When you adopt this way of thinking, you realize that every interaction with a coworker becomes customer service. Requests from inside customers are handled with the same speed and efficiency as those from outside customers. Carlos may never see or speak with the outside customers who do business with his organization, but he knows that his work affects someone who does. This level of service carries over to how internal phone calls are handled. Carlos handles calls from his coworkers with the same courtesy and professionalism as he would from callers outside the organization.

When answering calls from within your organization,

include the same elements you would when accepting calls from outside customers:

- **A friendly greeting.** This greeting should include where you are ("Warehouse"), who you are ("This is Carlos"), and conclude with showing a willingness to help the caller ("How may I help you?"). If you are not sure whether the call is coming from inside or outside the company, use the greeting you give outside customers, which should include your company name.

- **Prompt, courteous service.** Don't fall into the trap of giving only outside callers speedy service and putting internal customers on the back burner. Such prioritizing is dangerous because you may not be aware that your inside customer may be attempting to serve the needs of an outside customer. If you delay serving your inside customers, they can't help outside customers quickly.

- **Regular follow-up and follow-through.** Do you regularly call your outside customers to be sure their delivery arrived on time? Then why not also make such follow-up calls to your internal customers? Whenever possible, and practical, call or follow-up on requests from inside your company. Such follow-through can be carried out via e-mail or voice mail to increase efficiency. Carlos, for example, called the main office about one hour after the paper that had been requested was delivered. "It was a good thing I did," he recalls. "The paper had gone to the wrong area. If I hadn't followed up, I'd never have known. And the original person who called me would have wondered why I never sent the paper over."

Everyone at your company serves customers. Employees should be equally committed to serving customers across town and across the hall. Such continuous internal customer service can help you beat the competition.

SERVICE FROM THE INSIDE OUT

Although many of the ways you serve coworkers are the same as the ways you serve outside customers, there *are* ways your internal customers needs may be different.

What do our internal customers look for? Lynda C. McDermott, organizational consultant and author of *Caught in the Middle* (Simon & Schuster), offers five "basic quality indicators" that internal customers use to determine the value of coworkers' help. Internal customers, McDermott says, require that you:

1. provide or have access to the resources required to respond to their requests, including emergency or unforeseen needs;

2. respond quickly — or, better yet, immediately — to requests for information, services, or staffing;

3. accommodate your procedures and policies to their needs;

4. provide ongoing progress reports with no surprises; and

5. accept responsibility for problems and setbacks — then solve the problems.

SHARE INFORMATION
WITH INSIDE CUSTOMERS

No one would dispute the importance of good communication with the customers your company does business with. But what about the importance of communicating with your coworkers — those "customers" you serve within your organization? Information sharing can be a powerful tool to aid colleagues, helping them to do their jobs more easily with fewer errors in less time. It can also nurture a team approach to achieving a shared goal: satisfying the outside customer.

Use the following approaches to develop your information-sharing habit:

- **Capitalize on electronic mail.** If you have access to e-mail, send messages to one or more individuals at the same time. In less than five minutes, you can tell an entire network what you learned from an important customer, or how you solved a problem. For example, you may be able to identify items that are most popular with customers; when complaints are most likely (and from whom); and which suppliers respond to requests in a timely fashion.

- **Provide tips on job forms.** A California manufacturing firm encourages all those associated with a special job to write comments that will help everyone involved. Those in the warehouse, on the plant floor, and shipping and customer service employees share information about the customer, parts needed, problems encountered, and shipping arrangements. Group involvement through shared information leads to increased quality, productivity, and service.

- **Share articles of interest.** Route articles you think coworkers might like to read. Then everyone can benefit from your research. In some companies, articles, newsletters, announcements, and brochures are passed around and then filed for reference.

- **Use staff meetings.** Come to meetings with materials you may have obtained at a conference or trade show. Take the time before the meeting to highlight or underline what you think is important. Then briefly indicate what you will be circulating and why you feel it's worth reading.

- **Broadcast via the department bulletin board.** Have you ever come across suggestions on how to do a job more effectively? If company policy allows, post the item. The posting habit is a simple, cost-effective way to distribute information, especially if people are in the habit of checking the board.

- **Share personal experiences.** Let others learn from both your victories and your mistakes. Take a moment after a successful interaction with a supplier to let a coworker know what you learned. By sharing, you not only let others benefit from what you have learned, but they might share related information, too.

'FOCUS SHEET' SPELLS QUALITY COMMUNICATION

Know what you want to say, and what your reader wants or expects to learn. That's the cardinal rule for writing effective business communications, according to Sally Demler, a trainer with Better Communications. And whether you are communicating with internal or external customers, your written communication should reflect the quality you've built throughout your organization.

"Filling out a 'focus sheet' before you begin writing will help you stay on target," Demler says. A focus sheet helps organize your thoughts on paper before you begin writing. It should address four issues:

1. **The purpose of your communication.** Ask yourself two questions. First, "Why am I writing this?" You may be writing to persuade, request, inform, motivate, explain, recommend, praise, or announce. Second, "What do I want the reader to do?" Although your memo, letter, or report may be informational, Demler notes, chances are you also want your reader to take some sort of action.

2. Your audience. "You need to know if your reader will be receptive, indifferent, or resistant," says Demler. Knowledge of your reader also will tell you how technical you can be in your writing, and whether you need to "soft pedal" your message or be more assertive. On your focus sheet, answer these questions:

a. Who is my reader?

b. What does he/she already know about the subject?

c. How will the reader use this document?

d. How will the reader react?

3. The bottom line. "This is the key point you want the reader to remember," Demler explains. "If you can summarize this in one or two sentences on the focus sheet, you'll find it easier to write the entire document." Your key point isn't always the most obvious, such as, "We're having a meeting," Demler notes. You want the reader to know that, "This is a crucial meeting and it's important that you attend."

4. Strategy. The timing of your message must be right or it's futile. "If your intent is to solve a problem," Demler says, "make sure you're in time to deal with the situation. If you're too late, you're wasting your own and your reader's time — and damaging your credibility." A few strategy questions to ask:

a. Should I be writing this? At this time?

b. How should I distribute this document?

c. Should I consult with anyone before sending it?

d. Should I include a deadline for a response or action I expect my reader to take?

"In this age of information overload, the ability to stay focused in your writing helps ensure that your message will be read," notes Demler. Your focus sheet will help you do just that.

Avoiding Communication Pitfalls

Do you have trouble getting your message across to others? Do you misunderstand their messages? "Even if you were a perfect communicator you would still find yourself beset with communication problems due to the fact that you have to deal with all of us other imperfect communicators," says management consultant Michael LeBoeuf.

Communicating successfully takes effort. But you can become a more effective communicator by acknowledging the problems and pitfalls of communication and by finding ways to overcome them.

In his book *Working Smart* (Warner Books), LeBoeuf offers these guidelines for strengthening communication:

1. Recognize the inadequacy of communication. "Communication is a complicated, symbolic, abstract process with an unlimited number of things that can go wrong and that usually do," LeBoeuf says.

2. Think "existentially." "Remember that words are only symbols for reality in much the same way that maps represent territories," says LeBoeuf. "Frequently, things are not as they appear to be."

3. Find the total meaning in others' messages. "Don't just listen for words. Look for gestures, expressions, the sender's posture, and tone of voice," he advises. "And be conscious of these things when you are the sender."

4. Consider the source. "Who delivers a message is usually at least as important as what is said," explains LeBoeuf. The better you know your communicator, the more accurately you can assess message and motive. LeBoeuf says this recommendation is often ignored. "It's a good rule of thumb to remember that people will tell you what they want you to hear," he says.

5. Ask questions. "A lot of confusion can be nipped in the bud by asking someone to repeat or rephrase their statement," LeBoeuf says.

6. Be specific. "Illustrate your point," he says. Don't say, "You're causing us to miss our deadlines." Instead, say, "By starting your assignment so late and not giving it the time it needs, you are making the rest of the team fall behind schedule."

7. Communicate in everyday language. Don't use big words when there's a simpler way to say it.

8. Don't be afraid to say "I don't know." "Faking the answer only compounds the problems of ignorance," the author points out.

9. Be aware of nonverbal communication. "Punctuality communicates. Body language communicates. And silence communicates," says LeBoeuf. "You may be inadvertently sending wrong messages."

10. Be tactful. "The Christmas party isn't the place to ask the boss for a raise," says LeBoeuf. "Location and frame of mind have a great deal to do with how well ideas will be received and exchanged."

Finally, don't let all of these communication concerns stress you out! "A relaxed, open attitude will make people more receptive to your ideas and more willing to share their ideas with you," he says.

Maybe I Will and Maybe I Won't

The words you use make a big impression — on yourself as well as on other people. For example, don't water down a promise with the words, "I'll try." People who say, "I'll try to get this done by Thursday" are actually ducking responsibility for meeting deadlines and keeping promises.

"The project will be completed by Thursday" not only makes you sound self-confident, but it actually motivates you to live up to your word.[1]

Boss Should Top Your List of Customers

When you draw up a list of your biggest customers, place the name of your boss at the top. That advice comes from Philip B. Crosby, author of *Completeness: Quality in the 21st Century* (Dutton). Crosby is the father of the "zero-defects" quality concept.

"All of us have someone to whom we are responsible at work," he says. "The chairman has the board to worry about, the truck loader has the shipping supervisor. They are our customers because they lay out what we're going to do, and, of course, they have a major role in our completeness and job security."

For these reasons, Crosby asserts, relations are often tenuous between managers and their employees. For example, workers in many organizations think that the boss knows what to do. Meanwhile, the boss wonders about the problems of her employees. Better communication is essential to eliminate these questions.

Crosby says: "I learned to stick my head in the boss's office at least twice a week and ask if any problems with me had come up and if there was anything I could do to keep the boss happy.

---

[1] *From* Working Communicator *newsletter. (Lawrence Ragan Communications, Inc.)*

About once a month, I would drag my boss out of his office and on a tour of my area. This forced communication kept the boss feeling part of my operation. As a result, I was left alone."

ARE YOU SOFT ON QUALITY?

So, you're soft on quality?

That's good news for service and empowerment, according to Claus Moller, founder of San Francisco-based TMI North America, Inc. He draws a sharp distinction between "hard" and "soft" quality.

Hard quality refers to the technology finance, systems, methods, and mechanics of quality programs. At one time, this was the only side of quality that received any attention. Today, soft quality — which focuses on such "people" traits as creativity, flexibility, and empowerment — is getting more respect as an important part of the quality picture. In fact, TMI's soft approach has revived numerous "sick" companies through its "Putting People First" service-training program.

For example, British Airways' service was so poor that Britons began to refer to BA as "Bloody Awful." After one year of work with TMI, the airline increased its on-time takeoffs and landings by 23 percent, slashed customer complaints from 4 percent to .07 percent, and reduced employee absenteeism by 15 percent.

But before it can get passed on, soft quality has to start with you, the frontline employee. "Frontline workers play a crucial role because they're the first contact that people have with an organization," explains Leslie Wood, senior vice president for account management at TMI. For this reason, TMI has adopted an attitude of "employeeship."

"Employeeship means management by everyone. It allows you to align company and individual goals, take initiative and responsibility, implement change, and create higher-quality products and services," says Wood. Employeeship comes into play specifically during customer interactions, such as handling complaints. Wood calls this process "service recovery." You've been given ownership of the problem, and it's your task to follow through until the customer is satisfied. To do so, you must refine those soft quality skills.

Wood cites Moller's eight "golden rules" for handling complaints as a good place for you to start softening up:

1. Say "thank you."

2. Explain why you appreciate complaints.

3. Apologize for the mistake.

4. Promise to do something about the problem immediately.

5. Ask for the necessary information.

6. Correct the mistake promptly.

7. Check the customer's satisfaction.

8. Prevent future mistakes.

Says Wood: "Focusing on the customer, leading from the heart, and fostering a change in the culture are all 'people-first' strategies that will help your organization reach its goals."

'PARTNERING' HELPS UNCOVER NEW WAYS TO SERVE CUSTOMERS

You can't buy an insurance policy to guarantee your future, but you can adopt a concept called "partnering" as the next best thing. "Partnering is joining forces to deliver value to a customer," explains Eberhard E. Scheuing, author of *The Power of Strategic Partnering* (Productivity Press). The partnering process involves "getting into a customer's shoes" and seeing how you can work with others to satisfy the customer.

The possibilities for partnering are virtually unlimited, but the best place to begin your partnering process, suggests Scheuing, is with all of your internal customers and suppliers, your boss, and your teammates. Here are five steps to take toward partnering:

1. Look at the big picture. Go beyond your immediate responsibilities and develop an understanding of how you, your team, and your company all fit together to meet customers' needs.

2. Visit customers and suppliers. Site visits build relationships, says Scheuing. You can develop an understanding of who uses your product and how. And your customers actually learn to "see" you every time they receive the product. To get the most out of the visits, develop a purpose for the trip and an action plan to accomplish it. Make sure you and your teammates know what to look for and the kinds of questions to ask. And, gather the entire team together to "debrief" after the visit. Share observations and general thoughts, and decide how you can apply the information you've learned.

3. Participate in customer-focus groups. Customer-focus groups provide a forum in which to discuss customer requirements and needs. Some companies regularly convene customer- or supplier-focus groups. If your company doesn't, suggest having one to gain insight into customer needs. "It is very dangerous to think you know what your customers want and need, without really knowing for sure," advises Scheuing.

4. Get in touch with your boss's goals. Ask your boss how you can help achieve these objectives. Make sure your team and your personal goals are in alignment with those of your boss.

5. Visit your teammates as they work. Go to your peers and talk to them about their ideas for improvements. Ask questions, give feedback, and provide recognition for their work. The more you know about what your partners do — and the more you share about your own experiences — the more fulfilling your partnering experience will be.

THERE'S VALUE IN VALUES
IN QUALITY SERVICE

"Service improves when you attend to people's basic social needs," note Philip S. Wexler, W.A. (Bill) Adams, and Emily Bohn, Ph.D., authors of *The Quest for Service Quality* (Maxcomm Associates). "Among these are the need to be included, wanted, competent, and in control. This is possible only when you share and live by a set of well-articulated corporate values. Some companies have well-defined values spelled out in policy manuals," say the authors. "Others have never formulated or articulated their values, but they do exist."

The head of an enterprise is responsible for the values that influence employees. That's true in "top-to-bottom" hierarchies. However, the same principles apply to quality teams that have been empowered to operate in a "bottom-up" style.

Here's how some of the authors' theories apply to you and your teammates:

- **Training.** In some ways, a customer-service training program is similar to the treatment of an illness. A weak drug can cure if the patient has faith in the remedy. Conversely, a powerful drug will be ineffective if the patient doesn't take it as prescribed. If your employer has a training plan, he or she has shown the highest level of commitment to it. But it won't succeed unless the members of every quality team provide similar endorsement.

- **Quality substance.** In trying to stimulate service awareness, some management's launch quality drives with gimmicks such as banners, buttons, T-shirts, slogans, hats, and the like. There's nothing inherently wrong with such promotional aids if they generate enthusiasm. Even so, they represent only the form — rather than the substance — of quality service. An organization with a sound values system transmits it to people at every work level. Among frontliners, the message is clear: Treat your customers with the same courtesy that you expect.

- **"Walking the talk."** This term usually is applied to executives and managers who go out and "do" instead of remaining in their offices. You, too, can adopt an active attitude. When you serve a customer, don't just talk about what your company stands for. Walk your way to customer satisfaction through hard work and dedication.

- **Philosophical values.** H. Ross Perot outlined a code of philosophical-conduct values when he founded Perot Systems. In part, it reads:

  We will not tolerate anyone who acts in a manner which will bring discredit to the company; discriminates against another; looks down on others; or tries to move ahead at the expense of others.

Whatever your opinion of Perot as a politician may be, put it aside and study his code. It's what teamwork and values-oriented customer service are all about.

The service you provide daily to your customers, teammates, and supervisors will help define the quality of your work every day.

SELL QUALITY BY MAKING IT TANGIBLE

Your company is justifiably proud of the quality behind its products and services. But how do you "sell" quality to your customers? The intangible nature of quality has caused great difficulties for many professionals, including trainers, marketers, and, yes, salespeople. But there are ways to show people what quality is so they can reach out and touch it for themselves. Here are some suggestions to bring quality alive:

- **Demonstrations.** If you sell a product that can be demonstrated easily such as a computer, telephone, or photocopy machine, you must be able to show exactly what it can do and how easy it is to operate. Remember, your competitors probably have similar products with similar features. So find a way to distinguish yourself.

- **Guarantees.** Stand by what you sell. A company with a guarantee of "100 percent satisfaction or your money back" carries a lot of credibility. The guarantee is simple: If you don't like it, return it. No problem. But companies that have complex, confusing guarantees put off customers who think the company is trying to hide something.

- **Testimonials.** There is nothing more convincing than a company's competitor who is successfully using your product. Also, major clients such as Fortune 500 companies and federal and state governments, carry a lot of weight. Make the most of these special customers by asking for testimonials. Make it a point to use them at every opportunity.

- **Knowledge.** Quality salespeople need to know and understand their own business and their products or service. But more important is their understanding of the prospect's business. This is where you can differentiate yourself from others in the pack. Find out what the prospect wants rather than just talking about yourself and your company. Filling holes in the prospect's business will give you more credibility than a million flawless demonstrations.

- **Reputation.** If your reputation precedes you — and it's a good reputation — you're a step ahead. You can build one by using referrals and getting your name out in the industry. Take on speaking engagements, write articles, and get involved with professional organizations.

- **Flexibility.** Being able to roll with the punches is a valuable trait. As prospects throw objections your way, overcome them and answer all questions, responding quickly to objections and complaints.

QUALITY? DENTISTS RATE TOPS

What occupational group provides service of the highest quality? You may not be looking forward to your next appointment, but dentists rate as Number One. Airlines occupy last place.

Those are the key findings of a survey of 1,000 people conducted recently by the Gallup Organization and *Bank Advertising News*. Banks were in the middle of the pack. Gas and utility companies scored high marks. Physicians and hospitals were ranked just above airlines in the "worst" grouping.

The mid-level showing of banks surprised the pollsters. Jacques Murphy, senior vice president of the Gallup Organization, observes: "Given their emphasis on service quality, I expected banks to perform somewhat higher."

DON'T TRAMPLE ON CUSTOMER 'RIGHTS'

Customers are your most important asset. And, as such, they have certain rights and it's your job to uphold those rights. Richard A. Feinberg, head of Purdue University's department of consumer sciences and retailing, maintains that no quality-service program will succeed if any of these rights are trampled on.

So, in ascending order, here are your customers' top 10 rights and your top 10 service concerns:

10. Customers have the right to get what they want. "The days of 'If you build it, they will come' are gone," Feinberg says. "Businesses must start asking customers what they want and then give it to them."

9. Customers have the right to receive a "Wow." Because so many aspects of life are stressful, Feinberg contends, shopping for just about anything should be fun. You should provide service so incredible that patrons will exclaim: "Wow!"

8. Customers have the right to hear "Yes." Says Feinberg: "When customers are told that 'We can't do that,' they'll walk out and spend their money elsewhere. You must solve problems immediately."

7. Customers have a right to complain and get satisfaction. Consumers may be mad as hell, but many are still taking it. Soon, Feinberg warns, they won't tolerate it any longer and will seek revenge through patronage to your competitors.

6. Customers have the right to receive value. "People work hard for their money and want a product that's worth the price," the educator notes. "Shoppers will pay a premium to get quality."

5. Customers have the right to buy goods that work as promised. Too many product claims fall woefully short when put to the test. You should never suggest that an item will do something that's beyond its range.

4. Customers have the right to expect that everyone will work to serve them. Anyone who interacts with a customer represents the entire company. If you need help to meet your patrons' requests, ask for it.

3. Customers have the right to have it done properly the first time — and every time. "The biggest complaint about repair and delivery service is that it wasn't done right the first time," Feinberg says. "Nothing irks a customer more than to buy a defective product and waste time returning it."

2. Customers have the right to be treated with respect. For example, interrupting a sales transaction to answer the phone is rude and irresponsible. Work out a list of "service rules" to prevent such disrespect.

1. Customers have the right not to wait in line. Waiting wins the "bad-practice trophy" and rates as the No. 1 consumer complaint, Feinberg reports. "Everyone's time is precious," he asserts. "No one should be forced to wait more than a few minutes."

IDEA IN ACTION

MARRIOTT CHECKS IN ON QUALITY CUSTOMER SERVICE

Marriott has long been regarded as one of the premier hotel chains for good customer service. Yet, knowing that it could do still better, the hotel chain formed a team early in the 1990s to reach quality objectives. "Even though you've been successful, you still have to focus on the future and where the business is headed," notes Les Cappetta, Marriott Corporation's director of service development, in *Industry Week*.

The quality-improvement team brought together people from human resources, marketing, food-and-beverage service, operations, and engineering. Their mission was to redefine the meaning of good customer service.

Hotel patrons were asked what they consider most essential. The survey respondents revealed five key factors that influence their return trade: cleanliness, breakfast, friendliness of personnel, value, and check-in speed.

Marriott first zeroed in on its check-in practices. The survey team learned that guests define "check-in" as beginning when they make their reservations over the telephone. In their minds, it continues until they're settled in their rooms. Eighty-four percent said that the first 10 minutes of guest service determine their satisfaction level. Management now realized that a check-in overhaul was its most vital need.

The Marriott team selected check-in procedures on cruise ships as its benchmark. They move 1,000 people out and another 1,000 in with only three hours between departures. The group also studied the methods by which Hertz Corporation handles car rentals during peak time periods.

"The team measured front-desk activity and found that 75 percent of a desk clerk's time was involved in chores not related to check-in and check-out," notes *Industry Week*.

"These included providing services to and answering questions from other guests, opening and closing a shift, and resolving problems with reservations over the phone."

The removal of telephones from front desks did away with interruptions. And, one "guest-service associate" now does the work of a valet, doorman, bellman, front-desk clerk, and concierge.

According to Cappetta, 98 percent of all check-ins today take less than two minutes — almost a minute less than the average in 1990. Guests also rate the hospitality staff's attitude as improved.

FAST DELIVERY? SOLD!

How fast you deliver a product or service is often a significant factor in a potential customer's buying decision. Make sure you know your organizational delivery schedule, why delivery takes what it takes, and if and how exceptions can be made in emergency situations. No matter what your job function, you should make it your business to know.

THE CUSTOMER ISN'T ALWAYS RIGHT

Contrary to common thinking, the customer may not always be right, says Herb Kelleher, CEO of Southwest Airlines. That's hardly the answer you would expect from the head of the company that bills itself as the "Love Airline." But that's what Kelleher once told his employees.

According to *Incentive* magazine, Kelleher proclaimed this bit of counter-culture philosophy to show that he stands behind the decisions of his employees, which might include denying a customer a boarding pass. "I think you do an injustice to your people if you say the customer is always right. The guy who abuses our employee by yelling and screaming — is that person right? No! We tell them they are wrong and we don't want to carry them. Otherwise, you betray your folks," the airline CEO was quoted as saying.

This type of philosophy helped Southwest Airlines earn a spot in *The 100 Best Companies to Work for in America*.

Key point: Think about the needs of your customers — both internal and external. But use your good judgment if the customer wants something that is unethical or impossible.

QUICK TIPS

- **Keep a quality log.** When you get informal feedback (good or bad) about the quality of work you send to your internal customers, jot it down. Review your log periodically to see if you can spot trends that may require your attention.

- **Build in extra time.** When asked how quickly you can deliver something, ask for time to check. Find out how long it will take, add a day, and promise to have it there by that date. Then deliver it earlier. Your customer will be pleasantly surprised. Caution: Use this strategy on non-rush orders only!

- **Maximize tracking time.** Keep a list of the work schedules of your customers, including internal ones. List starting and quitting times, lunch hours, and busy periods. Include the best times to catch them at their desks. You'll spend less time trying to track people down and more time actually doing business with them.

- **Give complaints quick action.** Customers with complaints expect action within 48 hours, according to a survey by the Milwaukee Commerce Hot-Line. Also, most will put up with being transferred to a second employee — but not a third one. Do your best to respond much quicker than customers will tolerate.

- **Prioritize requests.** You've probably heard the saying: "You can't please everyone." But in business, only pleasing yourself isn't enough. To find a happy medium, make a list of the people who it's important that you please. This list may help you better prioritize the jobs and requests that come your way.

- **Put your quality commitment in writing.** The act of writing out your company's beliefs, policies, and goals — and how those apply to you — will help you better understand and appreciate this dedication to quality. Share this credo with customers to show you mean business.

QUIZ

DO CUSTOMERS QUESTION YOUR CREDIBILITY?

"My boss says that we need to improve our credibility with external customers and vendors. I've worked with a number of these customers for nearly a year now; I think that my customers all trust me now. How can I tell if someone is questioning my credibility?"

— T.A.L., Madison, Wisconsin

The three basic ways to win credibility are to earn it, to have it given to you by a referral, and to have it reflected on you through your product's or company's reputation. The first step in maintaining credibility is to know when customers are testing it. Assume that a customer makes each of the following statements. Then ask yourself in each case: "Is this a test of my credibility?" Write Yes or No after each question.

1. "I've never heard of you or your company. What can you tell me about your outfit?" _____

2. "Are you sure you can get this for me by the 15th? A lot depends on it getting here by then." _____

3. "What can you tell me about your competitors?" _____

4. "My banker tells me you're just starting out. Why should I trust my business to a novice?" _____

5. "Your company has a good reputation, but I don't know much about your product line. What can you tell me?" _____

6. "Would you like to know what your competition said about this same job? I've got the information right here." _____

SCORING: 1: NO. Since the person hasn't heard of you or your company — and mentions no referral — it's safe to assume that any credibility has yet to be established. And you can't lose what you don't have.

2: YES. This customer is testing your credibility. A lot is riding on what you've already told the person. This might be the ideal time to ask to use the phone and call your office or factory to guarantee the delivery.

3: YES. The customer is using a roundabout way to test you. The correct response is not to knock your competitors. Doing so tells people you don't have enough faith in your company and its products to let them stand on their own.

4: YES. This person already has a referral concerning you, so he or she is obviously interested. Your challenge is to prove you're not a novice.

5: YES. You're credible when you know about your product line — no matter what your job title is. The best response here might be: "Could you be more specific so that I won't cover material you're already familiar with?"

6: NO. This is a test of your integrity. Make it clear that you stand behind what your company stated, no matter what the competition had to say.

YOUR QUALITY TAKE-AWAY

The Second Simple Thing You Can Do for
Your Company and Your Career:

Be a *Super* Supplier to *Your* 'Customers'

In the old way of doing business, all the attention was focused on an organization's outside "paying" customer. Today, there is a realization that the better we serve each other inside the organization, the better we'll be able to serve all our outside customers. Companies utilize "partnering" programs as one way of "getting into the shoes" of internal and outside customers. Some, like Marriott, form quality-improvement teams to learn how they can best respond to their customer's needs. They also encourage communication within departments through training opportunities.

Not only will you become more indispensable to your organization when you strengthen the service you provide the customers inside your organization — you'll increase your worth in the job market, where the need for top-notch service providers is increasing.

What *You* Can Do

- Create a chart that helps identify internal customers. Serve them as conscientiously as you do your outside customers.
- Strengthen your writing and other communication skills.
- Take ownership of complaints and problems. Apologize for them and resolve them.
- Respond to requests with integrity.
- Respect all your customers' rights.

When you're a super supplier to the next person on your line, or to the department down the hall, or to the regional office 2,000 miles away, you're strengthening the links on the chain that eventually lead to your outside customers.

CHAPTER THREE

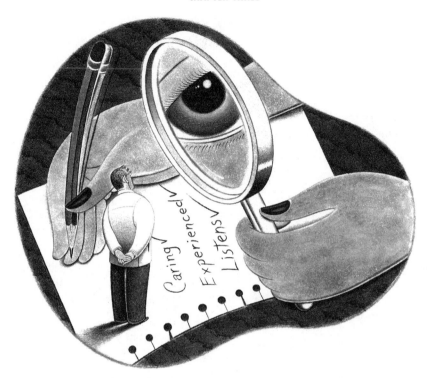

ZERO IN ON ZERO DEFECTS

"People forget how fast you did a job — but they remember how well you did it."
— HOWARD W. NEWTON (1903–1951),
AMERICAN ADVERTISING EXECUTIVE

Introduction

Zero defects is the goal of quality improvement programs run by most companies and departments. It's easy to understand why: Ask any manufacturing expert to name the biggest hindrance to productivity and profitability and this is what you're likely to hear: error, waste, and rework. Companies can regain enormous profits by reducing or eliminating errors.

But there is ample reason to be concerned personally about defects and error. Your ability to avoid errors greatly affects how you and others judge your personal quality. Errors can cause heavy costs and be the source of frustration and disappointment for yourself and for others.

It has been proven time and time again that preventing mistakes is much more time- and cost-effective than correcting them. You become much more valuable to your organization when you are zero-defects conscious. And you're making yourself much more desirable for any future position you pursue by having a cost-conscious attitude about the work you do today.

If we want to achieve a total-quality consciousness at work, we need to understand why mistakes occur, so they won't actually happen. The following are some of the most common circumstances under which accidents can occur, as identified by W.H. Weiss in *Production* magazine:

- When you are in a hurry to finish your work.

- When your mind wanders and you don't give the task at hand your complete attention.

- When you are tired and unable to think clearly.

- When you are upset, and you let it affect your attitude toward work.

- When you use the wrong tool for the job, or when you improperly use the right tool.

- When your work space becomes cluttered and unorganized.

If you recognize any of these situations in your own work habits, be careful — they can greatly inhibit your ability to do your job the best way you can.

Keep a list of one or two of your most common "mistake situations" in clear view. Then try to be more conscious of your attitude and surroundings at work. You may be more likely to stop yourself before you go too far the next time and ruin your quality record. And when you make mistakes, learn from them. Correct them. And don't allow yourself to make the same mistake twice.

How else can you zero in and on zero defects? The following information can help point the way.

'POKA-YOKES' SPOT DESIGN MISTAKES

The supervisor of your new product-development group said you should be "mistake-proofing" your new product at various stages of development. Why? And where do you begin?

People aren't perfect. For that reason, your product needs to be as close to perfect as possible. "Mistake-proofing," or including "catches" within the design of your product that prevent mistakes, will help.

Many products that you use daily are mistake-proofed. For example, if you drive to and from work, chances are you've left your headlights on once or twice after you left the car. Today, many cars are mistake-proofed with a bell or buzzer that goes off if you open your driver's side door or remove your ignition key with the lights still on.

Japanese quality guru Shigeo Shingo calls such devices "poka-yokes" from the Japanese *yokeru*, meaning to avoid and *poka*, meaning inadvertent errors, note authors Richard B. Chase and Douglas M. Steward in *Mistake-Proofing* (Productivity Press). There are four types of poka-yokes that your product-development group should consider:

- **Physical.** To identify errors, these mistake-proofers rely on a product's physical property or operation. It can be as simple as a template or a rule drawn around an area to indicate to customers where an item, such as a sticker or replacement part, should be placed.

- **Sequencing.** "Sequencing poka-yokes indicate, discourage, or prevent deviation from the order of steps in a process by making the completion of a later step contingent on an earlier one," say the authors. One such example is task substitution, which requires inserting steps to indirectly ensure that something will happen. Many guillotine presses, for example, require that the operator press two switches simultaneously, indirectly ensuring that the employee's hands are not in danger on the work area.

- **Grouping and counting.** This kind of stop-gap is designed to use natural groupings to make discrepancies stand out. Kits can help keep items together logically. Using checklists is a way to categorically group information so that omissions or additions are easily spotted.

- **Information.** These poka-yokes are used to get information that might otherwise be misplaced, forgotten, or ignored to the location where it can best prevent mistakes. Bulletin boards, customer mailings, e-mail messages, and more complicated computerized information systems can all assist in disseminating information.

Choose from any one of these ways to mistake-proof your new product.

THREE PROCESS FLAWS
THAT ENCOURAGE DEFECTS

Anthony Lynch, senior consultant to the manufacturing management unit of Arthur D. Little, Inc., of Cambridge, Massachusetts, says that the managements of many companies know what's required to improve quality. But, they often falter in putting needed measures into effect. He cites three common and critical mistakes. They are:

- **Failure to bring everyone together.** Lynch observes: "In a manufacturing organization, quality involves employees in design, engineering and processing, monitoring, and inspection. Too often, people responsible for one of these areas don't communicate with those responsible for the others." Work cooperation, Lynch stresses, must begin long before a product goes on-line. This is best done through teams composed of people at each production stage. The goal is to coordinate the product's design, engineering, manufacturing process, and quality assurance.

Lynch adds: "This approach to quality can be applied to companies that turn out almost any product or service. An ad agency, for example, may design a layout that looks great on the drawing board but fails in practice because it poses a difficult printing problem."

- **Poor monitoring.** Even with efficient monitoring machinery, quality can't be guaranteed. Lynch says it's essential to periodically remove a product from the manufacturing flow so that it can be examined for irregularities that usually aren't monitored. Overlooked defects often suggest much bigger production problems. As an analogy, Lynch notes that many wise home buyers first examine the quality of a house's molding. If the workmanship is poor, it probably indicates overall shoddy construction.

- **Imprecise checking procedures.** Says Lynch: "In the past, companies typically checked a product or part after it was made. Now, many realize that it must be inspected periodically between all manufacturing steps."

When these three flawed processes are corrected, you should emerge with a total solution. Moreover, the quality procedures used in manufacturing can apply to any business. By looking for defects along the way, you'll avoid creating products or services that turn out to be useless.

WATCH FOR 'WARUSA-KAGEN'

When you detect even the slightest deviation in equipment operations, stop and find out what's happening. If you fail to do so, an accident could occur.

The Japanese refer to such early-warning signs as *warusa-kagen*, says Michael Greif, author of *The Visible Factory* (Productivity Press). At the Tokai Rika plant in Japan, machinists are urged to report any *warusa-kagen*, or "quasi-problems" they encounter. Management has told them that the number of deviations they discover will indicate their observation capabilities. Within the first year that Tokai Rika workers launched their *warusa-kagen* detection campaign, 534 situations were reported. If they had gone unnoticed, Greif says, there would have been serious damage to equipment and possible injuries.

JIT: QUALITY, PEOPLE, AND 'DRUMBEAT'

"Just-In-Time" (JIT) is a highly effective, quality-building technique that many companies now are using to improve their operations.

JIT isn't new. It was pioneered by Toyota shortly after World War II but didn't reach North America until the 1980s. Then, the automotive industry and such innovators as Hewlett-Packard and Black & Decker put it to use.

With JIT, less becomes more. Production areas are streamlined and manned by small teams in work "cells." Inventory is cut to the bone through the delivery of supplies at the exact moment they're needed. Machinery is stopped whenever a problem arises, and the size of each production run is limited to a customer's immediate needs.

Charlene B. Adair-Heeley, author of *The Human Side of Just-In-Time* (AMACOM), pictures the JIT process as an industrial pyramid. The technical and procedural bricks comprise the top portion. They rest on three massive foundation blocks: quality, people, and "drumbeat."

If your employer implements a JIT program, here's how you and your teammates fit into its configuration:

- **Quality.** "Value-added" quality begins in the design and engineering stages but must also be present at every step until the finished product reaches the customer. "JIT is a state of mind, a philosophy," Adair-Heeley states. "It doesn't belong only to top management. The job belongs to you because you're the expert who knows more about your work than anyone else. You and the other experts must function as a team," she explains.

- **People.** Adair-Heeley lists these as the primary JIT objectives: beat the competition, create a culture of continuous improvement, involve everyone, eliminate waste, and strive for 100 percent quality. But these goals can't be attained by machinery alone: The key is people power. A redirection of energy may involve a transfer from your current position to one that calls for multiple skills.

  "There's a reduction for the line but not for the facility. JIT gives your company a stable workforce by shifting you to places where production is needed," she says.

- **Drumbeat.** This third foundation block consists of all the other internal procedures needed to make JIT work. They include production planning, scheduling, inventory control, and recordkeeping. Says Adair-Heeley: "You need a regular schedule that allows everyone — your team, management, suppliers, and customers — to 'march to the same drumbeat.' The ultimate goal is complete synchronization."

Team Approach Will Help Catch Errors Early

No matter how successful your quality team has been, you can't settle for the status quo. Like quality itself, teamwork constantly evolves. Peter R. Scholtes, author of *The Team Handbook* (Joiner), cites five tactics that will help your work unit attain continuous quality progress:

1. Maintain communication. The success of a project largely depends on how well your team members communicate with each other and anyone who will be affected by your work. "For instance," Scholtes says, "if a team is about to collect data from a working production line, team members should notify all supervisors and operators in advance. Tell them exactly why, how, and when the data will be collected. Similarly, a team studying how office employees use their time should explain that the goal is to identify inefficient systems, not people."

2. Fix obvious problems. As your team learns how to study processes, you'll uncover more problems that need fixing. Scholtes recommends that you explore each trouble area in depth. Gather data to support your belief that you've found an appropriate solution. If a problem is obvious and can be eliminated with ease now, go ahead and make the change. Don't wait until the entire project is completed. But, before you act, think ahead. What could happen if this solution doesn't work? How tricky and costly would it be to undo the change? Would that delay other activities?

3. Look upstream. "Most quality problems are only symptoms of other problems buried upstream in the process," Scholtes asserts. "For instance, variation in product quality may be the result of variations in raw materials. Mistakes in a customer's bill could be caused by errors in the original order or any steps in between." Scholtes recommends making long-lasting improvements by seeking out those causes and finding ways to prevent them. Also, when your team faces a problem, try to identify upstream conditions that may be the cause."

4. Document your problems and solutions. Some organizational problems are "solved" over and over again — after you try something that fails, you experiment with another solution. When that also falls short, somebody comes up with yet another idea. By documenting each attempt at a solution, real quality control can be achieved.

5. Monitor changes. "Rarely does something turn out exactly as you planned," Scholtes points out. "Though careful planning reduces the chances of unexpected problems, there's no guarantee. The only sensible plan is to monitor your actions so you can quickly catch errors and prevent them from becoming major problems."

TEAMS PARTNER TO SOLVE COMPANY-WIDE PROBLEMS

Production problems often manifest into other problems throughout an organization. That is why many companies are encouraging teams to partner with other departments and form specialty teams — or subteams — to research problems and develop encompassing solutions.

Pacific Bell, headquartered in San Francisco, did exactly that when it established the Cable Damage Prevention Project Team, composed of Pacific Bell employees from all over California, with members ranging from technicians to upper-level managers. The team was charged with decreasing damage to underground cable, of which there were 2,500 instances, totaling at least $4 million in repair costs in 1991. "Most of the damages were from nature, but others were caused by contractors and utility companies," says team leader Dan Brown.

By following a seven-step process for quality improvement, the Damage Prevention Team uncovered and solved the problems connected with the underground cable. The steps they used can benefit teams in any industry. See how this approach worked for Pacific Bell and think about how it might work for you:

1. Establish the reason for improvement. In this case, it's obvious: $4 million in repairs is a considerable expense.

2. Evaluate the situation. Before the team members could develop a strategy to solve Pacific Bell's damage problem, they needed to tabulate information to identify the source of the problems. Their research showed that 41 percent of the $4 million in damages was caused by contractors.

3. Evaluate the information. The team members analyzed their findings to pinpoint areas on which to focus preventive measures. They divided into seven smaller teams to address each focus issue, including customer awareness, legal issues, and Underground Service Alert (USA) procedures.

4. Create countermeasures. Through the subteam input, the entire team was able to use the information to establish four broad countermeasure areas: identification of underground cables, education of the public entities, easy process for work groups to identify damage, and technician-marking procedures.

5. Review the results. The team's work resulted in a 38 percent decrease in contractor-caused damage.

6. Standardize the solutions. By identifying all new underground cables with orange marking tape, Pacific Bell could alert contractors that they were digging where cables were buried, and prevent diggers from damaging them.

7. Set future plans. The final step in the team's process is ongoing. Future plans for keeping damaged cable rates down include education of and frequent contact with businesses that consistently damage cables.

Motorola's Journey to Be 99.9997% Defect-Free

Everyone connected with corporate quality knows that Motorola, Inc., has always been a forerunner in the quality movement. Fewer people, however, know how the electronics leader, based in Schaumburg, Illinois, reached the quality pinnacle. John Hillkirk and Gary Jacobson tell that story in *Grit, Guts, and Genius: True Tales of MegaSuccess* (Houghton Mifflin).

In 1988, Motorola beat 66 industrial rivals to take the Malcolm Baldrige National Quality Award for the 12.3-ounce Micro TAC, an almost defect-free cellular telephone that fits into a shirt pocket. The product didn't come out of Motorola's research laboratories in just a year or two. The company's quality push began in 1981 when chairman Robert Galvin and 80 other officers met to analyze the firm's market-share decline. During the discussion, one company veteran boldly criticized Motorola's quality. "That just electrified us," recalls Galvin. "At that one meeting, everything started to change."

The Motorola chief immediately appointed a quality director and set a seemingly impossible five-year objective: a tenfold reduction in defects. The quality staff spent two years inspecting the company's 24 factories. Plant managers got this message: If you have 5,000 defects per 1 million parts now, you must cut that to only 500 by 1986.

Quality was given top priority. When products didn't meet Motorola's new standards, shipments were delayed. Meanwhile, teams benchmarked at factories operated by such quality leaders as Matsushita and Seiko to learn their defect-control methods. Engineers reduced the likelihood of production errors by cutting the number of parts in each phone from 1,378 to 523. Hourly workers had the responsibility of identifying defects and were rewarded for their reports. Suppliers were told to improve their quality or lose Motorola's business.

By 1986, the company had achieved its goal: a 90 percent reduction in defects. The quality-control team then took on the challenge of attaining what became known as "Six Sigma quality." This meant that 99.9997 percent of the telephones would have to be defect-free. There could be no more than 3.4 flaws per 1 million parts.

The quality crusade soon spread to reach everyone. Executives attached beepers to their belts so that customers could reach them at any time. Company officers also visited customer facilities to talk with production personnel about problems involving Motorola equipment.

Today, the Motorola name is synonymous with quality.

HERE'S ONE WAY TO GUARANTEE ZERO DEFECTS!

At the onset of World War II, American Army paratroopers suffered from what can accurately be called a "quality problem." Some of their parachutes weren't opening. Not many were defective. In fact, if totals were kept and the number of non-opening parachutes were considered in comparison to the number that did open properly during a timespan of sufficient length, it could be shown that the number of failures was actually "well within variance." Variance, however, is a tough concept to explain to someone who is hurdling toward the ground.

The solution was to go to the parachute packers and — in today's vocabulary — involve them in what amounted to a tightly-focused quality process by saying, in essence, "Congratulations! From now on, every now and then, on a random basis, you get to jump ... using the last parachute you packed."

The percentage of correctly packed parachutes immediately jumped to 100 percent and stayed there throughout the war.

What Hazards Are Lurking at Work?

"Don't run in the halls!" is probably a familiar echo from your childhood. But the warning remains a valid office-safety rule today. The absence of easily recognized hazards often fools people into believing their office environments are completely safe. But danger can lurk around each blind corner and open file drawer.

Here are a few suggested safety rules to follow at your workplace:

- Use a lid to contain beverages that you carry to your work space.
- Walk, don't run to get that ringing phone.
- Check the "fish-eye" mirror for oncoming traffic at blind corners.
- Never leave a top file drawer open.
- Pick up all objects that fall — even a paper clip or piece of paper. They can create slipping hazards.
- Wipe up all spills.
- Store heavy objects flat to avoid getting your fingers crushed.
- Never wear loose chains, ties, or floppy sleeves around machinery with moving parts such as shredders and fans.
- Don't use a chair for a ladder.
- Stand away from doorways to avoid getting hit as a door opens or closes.

PRESCRIPTION FOR DISASTER

Wearing personal-protective equipment (PPE) is no guarantee against workplace injury — but not wearing it is an invitation to harm. Consider these data from the Bureau of Labor Statistics (BLS):

1. Hard hats were worn by only 16 percent of those workers who sustained head injuries, although 40 percent of them were required to wear this type of PPE in their work.

2. Only 1 percent of approximately 770 workers suffering face injuries were wearing face protection.

3. Only 23 percent of workers with foot injuries were wearing safety shoes or boots.

4. About 40 percent of the workers with eye injuries were wearing eye-protective equipment, such as safety glasses or goggles.

The majority of these workers were injured while performing their normal jobs at regular work sites.

OSHA requires engineering controls to be established as a first line of safety in a manufacturing environment. However, when hazards cannot be entirely eliminated through product or process engineering, OSHA standards require employers to furnish and employees to use suitable personal-protective equipment.

PPE should be used when there is a reasonable probability that injury can be prevented by using such equipment. If you notice a coworker not wearing the proper equipment on the job, explain how you don't want to visit him or her in the hospital.

TOTAL QUALITY CONTROL: IMPROVE THE THINGS YOU DO RIGHT

"Quality is what the user, the customer, says it is. ... Quality is a process. It is not a technical activity. It is not a set of seminars. It is not a set of statistics. It is a fundamental user requirement to user-satisfaction process that brings every man and woman in the organization into the service of quality.

"When I speak about quality, I'm not talking only about defects, the reduction of defects — zero or otherwise. That's not what it's about. What total quality control is about is increasing the number of good values that customers receive. That's the differential.

"Improve the things you do right; don't just cut down on the things you do wrong."

— DR. ARMAND FEIGENBAUM,
INTERVIEWED IN *INDUSTRY WEEK*

FORMULA FOR CONTINUOUS IMPROVEMENT INCLUDES STAFF SUGGESTIONS

Without new ideas, an organization can become stagnant — as a place to work and as a successful enterprise — or it can even become extinct. But where do the new ideas come from? Most often, they're generated by the people who do the actual jobs. Whether it's a formal program or simply an open-door policy, fostering a sense of enthusiasm and appreciation for new ideas can yield large dividends.

If you're thinking of proposing an idea:

- **Avoid proposing change merely for change's sake.** A suggestion should contain the promise of improvement — one that will save time and money. It should be a better way to do things, not just one that you would personally prefer.

- **Be prepared for skepticism.** Before you make a suggestion, think of every objection that might be raised. How could you respond with specific explanations? You might first consider trying out your idea on a coworker for additional insight.

- **Consider the timing.** You could kill the prospects for your excellent idea because your boss is distracted by other issues. Instead, request a meeting and tell the boss how much time you'll need.

- **Make your presentation professional.** You don't have to be overly formal, especially if your boss has a casual style. But you should be polished and concise. Ask for feedback, then listen carefully.

- **Support your case.** Bring in any background information that provides specific facts and figures to back up your argument. If yours is a cost-cutting idea, estimate how much money will be saved. If you can show tangible proof of where a similar idea actually worked, you'll strengthen your argument.

- **Remember that rejection is not the end of the world.** Don't pout or sulk. Instead, offer to continue to work on the problem and generate modifications of the idea. And don't assume that one rejection means that your boss won't be receptive to other ones. Keep all your ideas on file. What doesn't fly now might fly later — when the climate or staff has changed.

FOCUS ON ONE IMPROVEMENT AT A TIME

Your team is assigned to look for ways to improve productivity without increasing costs. It sounds like a good idea, but you don't know what to do.

Try these suggestions:

1. At your next team meeting, suggest that you and your coworkers focus on one improvement area at a time. Whether it's decreasing waste, improving safety building customer relations, or increasing work-flow efficiency, brainstorm with team members on how to improve.

2. Suggest that each team member develop at least one suggestion for an area of improvement, a means of implementation, and proposed results. Make sure that all suggestions are concrete, attainable, and ready by the next team meeting. Your team leader probably is already aware of some areas in which management would like to see changes made, so ask him or her for guidance.

3. When suggestions are made, discuss each one as a team. Ask: "How can I help implement that suggestion in my area?" "How much will it cost to make that change?" "What will the organization save as a result of this improvement?" The answers will help you decide which course of action to follow.

4. Be a team player when adopting the suggestions. You may not completely agree with the solutions, but each member of the team must be committed to what works best for the whole team if it is going to be successful.

As suggestions are implemented, do your part to make sure the changes are given a fair chance to succeed. If possible, bring up the results of the changes at each meeting and don't be afraid to make suggestions for making the improvements even better. As the positive results of your efforts begin to develop in one area, your teammates will be ready to make other improvements. And your team will be stronger for its efforts.

QUALITY IN GOOD TIMES AND IN BAD

Your team's vow to uphold quality should be for good times and bad. Quality isn't a "feel-good" tactic. It should be something ingrained in your team structure. Once it is, you won't need momentum to carry you through. "Momentum is not what keeps the quality process moving," says Philip B. Crosby, author of *Completeness: Quality for the 21st Century* (Dutton). "Necessity and success push quality along. Once people learn to work this way, they will not want to give it up. If something is worth doing, it will continue, regardless of temporary setbacks."

So, rather than accepting that poor profits indicate poor quality, set out to show how high quality can dictate high profits. Analyze how your team can contribute to raising profits in the future. Then get started working toward that goal.

QUICK TIPS

- **Identify defects.** Trying to identify the offending defect in a failing process? Look closely at areas of transition — when a process is moved from one machine or one person to another. Anytime attention must be diverted from the process itself to change machines or people, the chance for errors increases.

- **Set goals.** The act of setting a goal is more important than *how* a goal is set. Work groups with specific goals consistently outperform groups who are given a task and simply told to "do their best." For greater success, make specific goals that can be monitored.

- **Gradually improve.** You and your fellow team members should improve performance step by step instead of tackling too much at once. Then offer each other immediate feedback — both positive and negative — on each other's progress.

- **Celebrate often.** Don't limit team celebrations to major achievements. Marking lesser accomplishments can help motivate your team.

- **Don't ease up on quality efforts.** Ninety-eight percent of 127 government officials recently polled by Research and Forecasts, Inc., say quality is essential for the United States to retain a world leadership role.

- **Type it out.** Illegible handwriting is for doctors. If people can't read what you write, get in the habit or typing instructions or comments, so they won't be misconstrued. This is especially true when you're including numbers such as costs, dates, and figures.

- **Identify your weaknesses.** You'll strengthen your product or service quality when you ask a teammate to portray a salesperson while you pick on every possible weakness that comes to mind, suggests George Dovel in "The Best Readings" from *Business Marketing Magazine* (PWS-Kent Publishing).

LOOK BEFORE YOU LEAP INTO NEW PROJECTS

"When I sat down and analyzed the reasons for my mistakes and errors, I realized that most of my problems occur because I jump into projects without being fully prepared. I miss a deadline because I didn't fully understand the amount of work that would be involved, or some part of the project would need to be done because I did not listen carefully to instructions. What can I do to prevent such occurrences in the future?"

— K.W., Antioch, Illinois

Your ability to carry out tasks properly is a crucial element of your personal quality. Your chances for exciting, stimulating, and challenging new assignments and your opportunities for promotion largely depend on your ability to perform delegated tasks satisfactorily. You've made great progress by narrowing done where problems occur for you. Now begin taking the necessary steps to successfully launch your next new project. This quiz can set you on the right track. Write Yes or No after each question, then score yourself below.

1. Before accepting an assignment, do you make sure you understand completely what you are supposed to do? _____

2. Are the deadlines clear? _____

3. Is it clear how much responsibility and authority you have in the project? _____

4. Do you know which tasks you can perform on your own, without reporting back to your boss? _____

5. Do you let your boss know if a new assignment makes it difficult for you to do your other jobs? _____

6. Do you make suggestions to set priorities on how much time you will allow the project? _____

7. Do you get the information and background material you need to do the job properly? _____

8. Do you try to imagine all the problems and obstacles that could arise while you are doing the job — then plan accordingly? _____

9. Is it clear who makes decisions when your boss is not available? _____

10. If a problem arises that you can't handle, do you talk to your boss about the situation? _____

HOW DID YOU SCORE? If you answered nine or 10 questions as Yes, you are doing an excellent job of getting new projects off to the right start. Keep that up and you'll significantly lower the possibility for errors and mistake. If you scored any lower, take the corrective action explained in the questions you missed the next time you accept a project, and you'll be well on your way to performing your tasks more effectively.

YOUR QUALITY TAKE-AWAY

*The Third Simple Thing You Can Do for
Your Company and Your Career:*

Zero In on Zero Defects

Striving for zero defects is the cornerstone of all quality programs. People expect perfection and in many ways take it for granted; for example, if even only a one percent error level was allowable, there'd be 200,000 incorrect drug prescriptions filled each year, and no electricity, water, or heat for 15 minutes of each day. Organizations strive for zero defects by eliminating process flaws such as poor monitoring and imprecise checking measures. Manufacturing processes like just-in-time (JIT) help eliminate waste and create a culture of continuous improvement. Suggestion programs give employees an opportunity to find problems and offer solutions. Companies like Pacific Bell encourage teams to form partnerships with other teams to research problems and develop solutions. *Your ability to avoid errors greatly affects how you and others judge your personal quality.*

What *You* Can Do

- Check your work before handing it over. Try to locate the possible reasons for mistakes.

- Strive to remove the causes of defects and problems, not just the symptoms.

- Be happy when you discover a mistake. See it as an opportunity to prevent problems down the line.

- Wear protective equipment and avoid potential hazards.

- Don't compromise quality. No one should be afraid to jump with a parachute you packed and checked.

CHAPTER FOUR

REENGINEER YOUR THINKING

"The human mind, once stretched to a new idea, never goes back to its original dimension."
— OLIVER WENDELL HOLMES (1809–1894),
AMERICAN PHYSICIAN AND AUTHOR

INTRODUCTION

In a quality workplace, change is one of the few constants. Continuous improvement requires continuous reevaluation, which can mean the destruction of established ways and methods. In traditional work environments, managers have been trained to hold on to established ways of doing things. So the idea of "reengineering" your thinking and looking for new solutions can be a bit unsettling. However, when you look at the leaders in the quality movement — Malcolm Baldrige Quality Award winners like IBM, Ford Motor Company, and 3M — you see organizations that value and respect new ideas and fresh approaches.

Valuing contrary ideas is a principle that must be infused into an organization by its leaders and managers. Overcoming the barriers to new thinking is the true test of an organization's ability to adapt a quality philosophy.

A change in perspective starts with you. Your ability to adjust to changes and to look for new solutions to old problems will help you today and all along your career path.

One easy way to get started is by looking for all the ways you can challenge "the way things have always been done" thinking. On a personal level, taking a contrary approach can add challenge to your work or enhance your workplace success. Here are suggestions for contrary approaches that might work to your benefit:

- Work with someone with whom you've had difficulty before. In today's smaller, downsized offices or team environments, it's tough to avoid people with whom you might have had run-ins, arguments, or just "bad chemistry" before. Instead of expending the effort to avoid contact, try to work cooperatively with that person. By challenging your own prejudices, keeping an open mind, and demonstrating your own positive attitude, you can forge a workable (or even good) relationship.

- Volunteer for a task that "scares" you. Is there a job that always has intimidated you because you thought it was beyond you, required too much work, or seemed too risky and challenging? Take a deep breath and volunteer to do it. One excellent way to achieve personal and professional growth is to stretch your limits and put your abilities to the test. More often than not, your impression of your own inadequacies will prove wrong — and you will live up to the challenge and succeed. But you'll never know if you don't try.

- Learn a new, completely different skill. Have numbers always frightened (or bored) you? Take an accounting course or learn how to use a spreadsheet program. Practice your writing skills. Could a second language help you advance? Why not check out a Spanish or French class at the local community college?

- Don't play office politics. Sure, there's a perverse kind of allure to listening to rumors and innuendoes about your managers and colleagues. But you will be much better off if you avoid gossip. Stay out of things that aren't your personal business, and be open and up front in all your business dealings.

- Avoid telling bosses just what they want to hear. As Abe Lincoln said, honesty is the best policy. This also applies to the workplace. Be honest, though not brutal, when responding to questions or requests for feedback. Offering empty flattery or downright lies might produce results in the short term, but eventually they won't get you or the company anywhere. Though an honest response may not bring a smile, it will enhance your reputation for integrity. You'll be valued far more for your candor than for any abilities to con others.

Taking the road less traveled may not always get you where you want to go, but there are plenty of situations where taking a contrary approach will lead you to a better destination. What other techniques can you utilize to reengineer your thinking? The following suggestions can show you.

What Would You Do?

Technology Isn't Always the Answer

Each time a company experiences a quality problem, someone is quick to throw technology at it to "make it better." This Band-Aid approach doesn't seem to address the real problems.

The incessant promotion of high-tech solutions to quality challenges has become very appealing. However, after installing a new high-tech system that promises to be "the answer," frequently a company's productivity drops, flexibility decreases, and employee morale deteriorates, says Charles N. High, president of High Dynamics Company, an Augusta, Georgia-based planning and marketing management company. In such cases, the same people who have reengineered their thinking to find technology solutions sometimes need to think again.

So, what's wrong? Simply this: It's much easier to throw money at a new technology than it is to determine and address the root causes of quality problems. "Instead of focusing on the real issues, people sometimes 'buy' a high-tech answer because it looks good and just hope it is 'on target,'" says High. "If it is not, the 'techno-answer' then becomes a scapegoat for the real solution and often obscures the original problem."

Before turning to technology as the response to the next quality challenge, High suggests first asking these six questions as a means of getting at the core issues:

1. Do we define and address specific issues and problems that directly affect our business success?

2. Do we solve real problems or skirt them?

3. Do we need to change our management style, people, or corporate structure?

4. Do we objectively understand our company's major strengths and build success on those strengths?

5. Do we know what our critical weaknesses are and correct them?

6. How effectively do we make decisions and communicate with the affected employees?

Experience tells us that business systems often have problems and fail because we fail to manage those systems — not because there are any technical problems, says High. We must effectively manage our quality programs by knowing what the critical factors are and being prepared to focus our energies to meet challenges as they arise, he says. "Only then should we pursue the assistance of technology and only to make the achievement of our quality goals more efficient."

TEAM TASKS HELP INDIVIDUALS REFINE THEIR STYLE

Working together as a group toward a common goal challenges all participants to refine their individual working styles. The demands of the task at hand need to be framed from the perspective of all members of the group.

A team needs to use certain "task behaviors" to accomplish shared projects, according to Ken Blanchard, coauthor of the monograph, *Fundamentals of Effective Teamwork* (Blanchard Training and Development, Inc).

Here are several task behaviors your team should try to develop:

- **Initiating.** Propose new topics or suggest different

courses of action. ("Let's take a look at some of our options ... ")

- **Information seeking and giving.** Solicit ideas from others, and offer your own. ("John, considering your experience, what would you suggest?")

- **Clarifying and elaborating.** Interpret suggestions, define terms, and build on ideas. ("That sounds workable, John, and we also might be able to ... ")

- **Summarizing.** Present information in an understandable form. ("To summarize what we've talked about ... ")

- **Consensus testing.** Check for agreement, or evaluate a decision. ("Are we all in agreement that ... ?")

- **Coordinating.** Manage the flow of information. ("Let's hear what everyone has to say before we ... ")

'Right' Questions Will Reframe Your Way of Thinking

Good quality campaigns hinge on good questions. Unless you and your teammates know how to ask the right kind of questions, you won't uncover problem areas or identify improvements. You also won't gain employee or management buy-in to your system; thus, company growth will be stunted. "Dramatic improvements [occur] not by teaching people new skills but by asking them different kinds of questions. ... questions that create ownership for the improvements you want," notes Doug Krug, coauthor with Ed Oakley of *Enlightened Leadership* (Simon & Schuster).

But not all questions are helpful. Those that put people on the defensive only serve to undermine morale and productivity. For example, the question, "Why did that mistake happen?" focuses attention on placing blame. It's much better to ask,

"How can we solve this problem?" to place emphasis on making things right.

Questions phrased in a positive way build feelings of empowerment, generate trust, and foster creativity. The authors offer these guidelines for effective quality questioning:

1. Ask open-ended questions. Avoid any question that will elicit a "yes" or "no" response since these won't shed light on the reasons things happen. For example, instead of asking, "Do you agree with this statement?" ask, "What do you think about this?"

2. Focus on the future. Don't dwell on something that's already happened. Instead ask, "What do we need to do to get where we want to be?"

3. Concentrate on "what" and "how" issues. "Why" questions are likely to bring forth justifications. This approach is much better: "What process did you use to make that decision?"

4. Know that there are no wrong answers. Even if you don't agree with a team member's opinion, remember that he or she thinks it's correct. Again, use "what" and "how" questions to find out how they arrived at their decisions.

5. Consider each answer. Don't conclude that yours is the only solution to a problem. Hear what peers have to say, and weigh the alternatives.

6. Listen. Don't become so preoccupied with thinking up good questions that you don't listen to the answers.

7. Avoid misunderstandings. The wrong question can build a wall of mistrust between teammates. Be clear about why you're seeking certain information.

Remember that the purpose of questioning is to gain information. The most effective questions, Krug says, are those that convey this message: "You already have the answers. Please tell me what they are."

GO WITH 'FLOW' TO REACH QUALITY GOALS

Try to recall whether your quality team ever experienced this: You had a tough deadline, put in many hours of overtime, and finally made it under the wire. Everyone should have collapsed in exhaustion. Instead, you all broke out in laughter. It was, in fact, the start of a celebration. You realized that your team had reached its success pinnacle. At least for a time, you and your teammates had become "superachievers." How did you do it? It's simple. Everyone in your work unit was in *flow*.

"Flow is the secret of superachievers. It's a sense of concentration so total that everything but your work ceases to exist, and time seems to stand still," writes Srikumar S. Rao, a professor of marketing at Long Island University in New York, in *Success*. "Successful people have always known instinctively how to reach this state. Now, psychologists have provided a road map that lets anyone with discipline and ambition achieve it at will," Rao points out.

The concept of flow was introduced by Mihaly Csikszentmihalyi. In his clinical studies at the University of Chicago, the psychologist analyzed top executives, star athletes, famous artists, and superachievers in many other fields. He devised a six-step procedure to reach a state of flow. Its components are:

- **Gamesmanship.** "Nothing rivets concentration like the thrill of competition," Rao asserts. "Exploit this force to its fullest. A game has rules, a clearly defined outcome, methods of measuring progress, penalties, and rewards."

- **A powerful goal.** Financial objectives aren't sufficient, Rao says. They won't generate flow. You need an overwhelming *spiritual* goal that will bring meaning to your work. Rao tells of a friend who is a highly successful insurance agent. He found his flow because he believed that, through his product, he could help people.

- **Focus.** The marketing scholar stresses that you must eliminate all distractions. To think effectively your team must set aside specific blocks of time. Put away all thoughts of personal matters. They are, Rao contends, "like the tiny beetles that can fell a giant redwood." His advice: Squash them.

- **Surrender.** This step is the most difficult. If you really want to attain a goal, it's natural to *strive* for it. Don't do it. Pushing, Rao says, will lead to anxiety. The search for flow no longer will be a game. "Let go," Rao urges. "In flow, the world works *with* you."

- **Ecstasy.** By following the previous steps, ecstasy will be the natural result. It will overtake you by surprise. At first, you won't know what hit you. But, soon, there will be no mistaking it. You have reached the threshold of flow.

- **Peak productivity.** Flow will envelop your entire team. Says Rao: "Your ecstatic state will open vast reservoirs of resourcefulness, creativity, and energy. Your productivity and quality of work will shoot through the roof."

THE PAUSE THAT REFRESHES THINKING: CONCENTRATION MOMENTS

The phone is ringing; the computer printer is clattering away; your officemates are discussing policy changes; and you have to finish proofing project notes before your 10 a.m. meeting. Just a typical morning at work. What you wish for is a big, soundproof door to close out all your distractions. What you need is a "concentration moment."

Concentrating so completely on a project at hand while a busy office whirls around you is the skill of a fine-tuned professional. According to psychologists, this high level of mental effort is actually a form of self-stress. An individual focuses so completely on one task that becoming distracted is less likely, and working hard to get a job done quickly and well is the desirable result.

As the center of many activities in your office, finding lengthy periods to concentrate will be unlikely. You can, however, find moments during the day when you can get important work done. In five-to-15-minute periods set aside for intensity, much can be accomplished. When those periods occur will depend on your work schedule as well as your own body clock. Ask yourself when you're at your most productive and see if you can arrange your concentration schedule around that.

Where you work is also important to your ability to concentrate. When others are not around and the phone is less likely to ring — say, between 12 p.m. and 1 p.m. — you may be able to give work the undivided attention needed to truly concentrate. You also may want to find a location away from your normal work area to focus on some tasks. Try finding an empty office or a conference room to occupy for a time.

Once your schedule and your environment are attended to, you can begin the process that will help you focus intensely. To create and foster concentration moments:

1. Make a list of what you want to accomplish. If you have only five minutes to spare, make it a mental list. The list-making method begins the process of shutting out other items and distractions.

2. Select one item to begin your concentration moment with. Organize the material you need to finish so you have no excuse to get up to retrieve your files or supplies.

3. Pause to relax before you begin. Closing your eyes for even a few seconds can help clear your mind, which is essential

to concentration. Taking a few deep breaths can also help accomplish this.

4. Commit yourself to always getting one job done before you stop. Direct yourself to concentrated effort with a message such as "I won't stop until the monthly sales report is finished." Then, let distractions wait until you meet that goal. If you have trouble with this stage, make your goals smaller and more manageable so that you always experience that important feeling of accomplishment.

Concentration moments can become positive addictions, says psychiatrist William Glasser. They produce such useful and valuable results that you'll want to keep having them. Eventually, these moments will become a routine for concentrating that is comfortable as well as effective.

Every great success is made up of many concentration moments. So, when you start to feel overwhelmed by your workload, measure your success one moment at a time.

GET INTO A CREATIVITY MINDSET

Quality and creativity are so closely linked that it's almost impossible to think of them separately. Your team needs innovative methods to solve problems, make decisions, and achieve your organization's overall goals and mission. But creativity isn't something you pick up in your workplace and then discard when you go home.

A creative mind opens along with the eyes each morning, says Art Cornwell, author of *Freeing the Corporate Mind: How to Spur Innovation in Business* (Execu-Press). Further, it's active throughout the day and well into the night. Cornwell has a formula that's designed to help you keep a crisp mental outlook in every aspect of your life with a minimum of effort. These are his creativity-generating tips:

- **Change your morning routine.** "Each of us has a routine that we follow in the morning," he observes. "These routines are so well established that we really don't have to think at all before we get to work.

  "Your mind is basically asleep. Wake it up! For example, if you eat breakfast at home, eat out. If you follow a particular route to work, find another one. Do something different to get your mind moving earlier."

- **Analyze at least one problem each day.** Aside from team problem solving, use your own ingenuity to think of unique ways to accomplish work procedures. Even if it "ain't broke," fix it. Look around your office or plant. What could be done better? Think about it during the day, and try to reach a conclusion. Tomorrow, take on another challenge. This exercise will not only boost your creativity, but also give you a daily sense of accomplishment.

- **Be a "know-it-all" at something.** Says Cornwell: "Innovative ideas aren't produced at random from some unknown stockpile of data. They're actually a merger of ideas from dissimilar fields of experience. A person with many interests tends to be more creative; he or she has a larger knowledge base from which to work. Select a field in which you're already interested, and invest your time in learning more."

- **Pretend this is your first day on the job.** When you first joined your team, you may have seen something you wanted to change. Now, with time, you've become accustomed to the status quo. When you go to work tomorrow, let your mind return to those early days. Take advantage of your experience; look again for an area that needs improvement; and share your thoughts and ideas with your teammates. Don't let yourself get stuck in a workplace rut.

- **Find at least three alternative solutions to any problem.** "You already have one solution to every situation, the one 'right' answer," Cornwell notes. "However, you can't stop there. You need at least three. Each new solution will take you in different directions. New options, new alternatives will open to you and your teammates." Besides, it's always good to have a backup plan.

- **On a daily basis, ask "What if ... ?"** This is a simple technique, and it's fun. Once a day, examine a workplace situation and ask yourself: "What if ... ?" Follow the phrase with a statement that's either false or only partly true. Through a bit of whimsy, you'll reach some interesting conclusions.

- **Practice!** "Thinking creatively is much like learning long division," Cornwell says. "When your teacher first described the process, you wanted to avoid it entirely. But soon, you began following instructions. Through constant repetition, you learned how to do it. The same is true of creative teamwork. Practice, practice, practice!"

JUMP-START QUALITY WITH CREATIVITY

Are you caught up in a daily routine? If you can accurately predict how your day will go — from what you're going to eat at lunch to the results of your quality checkup, then you may need to expand your creativity horizons.

Creative people tend to take more risks at work. They have a reputation for being "can-doers" and solution-finders. They're always going on about new approaches and ways to improve quality.

Creativity will not only improve your work, but you'll find yourself enjoying it more as well. Here are a few ways to make yourself more creative:

1. Broaden your horizons. You can't get new ideas by doing the same things day in and day out. This doesn't mean that you have to take up skydiving. But how about using a new work tool or trying a new procedure?

2. Take a new approach. A different perspective to an old problem can offer you new solutions. Why not explore how your peers solve quality problems that frustrate you?

3. Challenge your assumptions. Just because you've done a task a certain way for a period of time doesn't mean it can't be improved. Don't assume that what you're doing is right. Prove the effectiveness of your methods and procedures to customers.

FOCUS ON MAKING CUSTOMERS *UN*-HAPPY (YES, YOU READ THAT RIGHT!)

Do you know how to completely ruin the quality of your service so that customers hurry away, never to return? You should if you hope to succeed. Sometimes the best way to meet your customers' service expectations is to reverse your thinking. Focus on what they don't want, says quality pioneer Philip B. Crosby. He has been dispensing no-nonsense quality advice ever since he introduced the "zero-defects" concept years ago.

Crosby suggests making a list of these customer quality killers. "Consider each item in terms of how we would make certain that customers did not receive what they wanted. This lets us learn how to prevent problems by seeing what's necessary to create them," he says.

For example, let's say your quality team operates a hotel. How can you treat your patrons so badly that they'll never return? The process begins at the registration level. Never send a confirmation in writing. That gives people the assurance that a room will be waiting for them.

Be sure that all the parking spaces near the hotel are

occupied by employees. When your visitors locate the unmarked registration desk, the clerk should be tied up on a personal telephone conversation. When check-in finally takes place, quote a much higher price than "promised."

Give your guests plastic electronic keys that won't work and wave them in the general direction of the elevators. When they return to the desk to report the defective keys, tell them they're doing it wrong. When they do get in the room, have them greeted with a scream from the undressed person who hasn't checked out yet.

The room should be much smaller than those pictured in your advertising flyer, and soap and other personal items should be tightly rationed.

Thinking out of the box in this way — to establish the ways of making absolutely certain that customers are unhappy — will bring forth your teammates' creativity, says Crosby. "They'll look at the company in an entirely different way and from a very different point of view. They'll redesign the system to suit customers' needs."

LET THE (QUALITY) REVOLUTION BEGIN!

People who are committed to total-quality management (TQM) can learn from Third World revolutionary leaders. Warren H. Schmidt and Jerome P Finnigan, authors of *The Race Without a Finish Line* (Jossey-Bass), contend that revolutions are most successful when they're led by those who can inspire others to follow them. They draw these analogies to TQM:

1. Revolutionaries seek to change society's laws and regulations. In TQM, change is aimed at organizational standards and measures.

2. Recognition and reward systems create loyalty among political revolutionaries and TQM advocates alike.

3. Control of the mass media is essential to any revolutionary army. In TQM, communication of quality messages is equally important.

4. Revolutionaries rely on universities and other schools to spread their way of thinking. TQM needs educational programs to bring about a smooth transition.

5. Leadership and commitment are critical in both revolutionary armies and quality-attuned organizations.

6. When the battles are over, a select and dedicated group of experts supervises change. Comparable organizational structures and roles are needed to attain TQM objectives.

Let the revolution begin!

ADAPT AS BUSINESS CLIMATES CHANGE

The face of global business has changed significantly in the 1990s. Increasing competition from both domestic and foreign companies, coupled with the recent recession has forced many businesses to become "leaner and meaner."

The shrinking of business and service organizations may be more than a one-time occurrence, according to Louis S. Richman in *Fortune* magazine. Rather, this "decruiting," as some executives choose to call it, may be a long-term trend. In some business arenas, there seems to be a competitive "my workforce is smaller than yours" rivalry taking place, says Richman.

Are organizational changes in your company's future? No job holds a guarantee these days, so here are some strategies for reengineering your own thinking to adjust (and thrive) during company turmoil:

- **Understand your company environment.** Make it your business to be up-to-date on the state of your company's industry and its competition. Based on these factors, company executives will be making important operating decisions that will affect you. If you keep abreast of developments, you will have a head start in knowing what to expect and will be able to brace yourself for sudden changes.

- **Expand your horizons.** Knowledge of the outside environment will allow you to develop proactive suggestions to head off problems or take advantage of opportunities you might foresee. At the very least, your keen awareness enhances your value to the organization.

- **Listen to management.** If your company is gearing up for change, management will probably communicate the direction in which it is headed, what needs to be done to effect the change, and what it expects from employees. If you're unsure about your department, your role, or proposed changes, ask someone. You can't find a niche in management's game plan if you don't understand the decisions it makes.

- **Know your survival skills.** Top managers going through change (or even chaos) cite traits that can help employees survive: demonstrating a flexibility of skills and a concern for quality. Other specific technical skills might increase your value as well. If ever there were a time to seek out more education and training, this is it.

- **Replace fear with enthusiasm.** It's only natural to feel uneasy when rapid changes occur in your job. However, focusing on your fear will only throw you for a loop — and might lead to fatal mistakes if you're afraid of taking risks. Instead, make a conscious effort to look at this as a time of excitement.

The status quo is probably gone for good, so let go of it. Allow yourself to enjoy playing a part in the creating of something fresh and new. It might be a little scary, but most things that are worthwhile usually are.

IDEA IN ACTION

MARS' QUALITY METHODS ARE
OUT OF THIS WORLD

Mars is known as the red planet. At Mars, Inc., the candy maker, quality levels are so high that they may well have come from outer space. Based in McLean, Virginia, a corporate staff of only 50 oversees a worldwide workforce of 25,000. Mars also produces pet food, rice, and other consumables.

Craig J. Cantoni, a human resources executive in New Jersey who previously worked for Mars, recently described the company's atmosphere in a *Wall Street Journal* article:

> Mars is secretive and closely held. Being hired from a conventional publicly-held company is akin to an earthling trying to survive on the red planet. You must let go of most of the beliefs and assumptions learned in a normal business environment.

> The first visible symbols of this alien culture are the absence of assigned parking spaces, private offices, or even partitions between desks. ... Everybody punches in, including senior executives and the billionaire owners.

Frequent impromptu meetings, beehive activity, and direct communication are the norm at any Mars office or factory. Nobody writes memos or uses electronic mail.

Everyone is "connected." Every office is connected to a plant. There, workers and managers alike wear white uniforms and "bump" hats. The facilities are spotless; the lines run at high speed; and everyone is loyal, proud, and well-paid.

When one of the Mars brothers shows up at a subsidiary, he heads straight for the plant and dons a white smock and bump hat. Cantoni reports: "Woe to the plant vice president if less-than-perfect product is coming off the line. Quality is an unrelenting obsession at Mars. One example is a fear of 'incremental degradation,' a term used by Mars to describe what can happen by using cheaper ingredients."

Everything — including pet food — is tasted. A few tiny and nearly invisible chocolate-coating nicks can result in the tossing out of an entire production run of candy bars.

Mars operates with 30 percent fewer employees than its closest competitor. There are only six pay levels. Nearly every general manager has worked extensively in marketing or manufacturing in at least two Mars facilities.

Says Cantoni: "Companies like Mars can force us to face the possibility that we are wrong about what a true quality culture looks like. Instead of looking overseas for answers, maybe we should look to another planet. The Mars Voyager is waiting on the launch pad."

<u>IDEA IN ACTION</u>

COST-CUTTING DURING A CRISIS

During an economic recession, organizations of all sizes face an immense challenge. They try to cut operating costs without reducing their workforce, slashing payrolls, or increasing errors. While you strive to maintain the quality of your own work, it's also essential to seek out top-quality and low-priced suppliers.

That may require a reengineered approach. Quill Corporation in Lincolnshire, Illinois, is one of the nation's largest mail-order office product distributors. Worldwide, it has some 800,000 customers. Quill recently published a new edition of its booklet, *How to Save Money on Office Supplies*. Among numerous expense-chopping tips, Quill focuses on the process of selecting suppliers.

Even if you're not involved in purchasing, you can watch

for areas in your department where money can be saved. Then, pass your findings on to your manager or purchasing director. Here are Quill's guidelines:

1. Evaluate your buying frequency. Big companies in metropolitan areas usually get the best price deals because of volume buying. Nevertheless, small firms also can secure significant savings. "Consolidating your orders will save you time and give you the money-saving benefits of buying in large quantities," Quill advises. "In addition, by knowing what you need and when you need it, you will be able to take advantage of periodic sale prices."

2. Determine your primary supply needs. As you and your quality-group associates go about your daily tasks, maintain a log of the supplies you use each day or week. Your purchasing director will then be able to decide what and when to buy from a "one-stop" supplier. Quill cites these advantages in using a single supply source: explicit pricing, overall good values, superior service, helpful personnel, stability, consistency, convenience, and time saving.

3. Chart your special-buy requirements. An accounting department will have different needs than, say, an engineering group. Keep track of how much out-of-the-ordinary supplies you use. By pinpointing your specialized-product volume, Quill explains, your purchasing chief can save money by locating the best secondary supplier. Such houses also are reliable sources for rush shipments.

4. Rate your supplier's quality. The Quill booklet notes: "Suppliers should be tested on each step in the process of placing, receiving, and (when necessary) returning orders. "A good supplier will guarantee 100 percent satisfaction. As a customer, you shouldn't settle for anything less. If you aren't satisfied, then you didn't get a good deal." Keep your purchasing office advised on such matters as quality, timeliness of deliveries, and willingness to make exchanges or accept returns.

Product substitutions also can result in substantial savings. For example, when Northeast Utilities installed new energy-efficient fluorescent bulbs last year, it saved Connecticut businesses $4 million.

'LITTLE TICKET' COST-SAVING IDEAS

Cost-improvement goals are commonly assigned to supervisors. But if your company has been on a mission of continuous improvement for several years, you may be wondering how you can come up with ideas to cut costs, since all of the "big-ticket" items seem to be gone. The solution: Look for savings in "little-ticket" items. Here are some ideas suggested by Jerry Bolnick, of Common Business Systems, Inc., in *Boardroom Reports*:

- Review the business forms your department uses. Eliminate sections on multipart forms that are no longer used. Savings can come from reduced printing costs (half-page vs. whole-page documents) and possibly reduced postage costs. Plus, it takes less time to complete shorter forms.

- Ask vendors to store inventory for your company. This saves storage space that could be used for productivity-centered activities.

- Convert high-volume forms to self-mailers, if possible. Savings come from not having to fold, seal, and stamp outgoing invoices and statements.

- Find out who doesn't use regularly-produced reports, such as daily production reports. Eliminate them from the normal distribution channel for savings in paper and clerical time.

- Use a fax stamp instead of a separate fax cover sheet.

- Make your own self-stick notes by using a special glue stick and scrap paper.

Just as You Always Expected: One-Third of Meetings Are a Waste of Time

At any time during the working day, more than 2 million meetings are going on in American workplaces. Experts say up to one-third of those are totally useless — two out of three fail to meet their objectives. Attendees of many of those meetings are likely to agree.

These are among the findings of a recent survey conducted by Hofstra University in Hempstead, New York. Fortunately, the study also concluded that the skills needed to make these meetings better can be acquired through training. One popular source for meeting training is *More Bloody Meetings*, British comedian John Cleese's sequel to *Meetings, Bloody Meetings*, both produced by Video Arts, Inc. Cleese uses his trademark humor and wit to give some seriously effective advice for better meetings:

1. Make sure a meeting is necessary. If there aren't enough agenda items to justify one, cancel it.

2. Pay attention to seating. In particular, don't place potential antagonists directly across from one another. Also, separating close partners can help foster more independent thinking.

3. Expect five types of attendees: aggressive, silent, abusive, rambling, and sniping.

4. Lighten the meeting agenda with good-natured humor. A humorous anecdote can be an effective catalyst for creative brainstorming.

5. Embarrass latecomers by locking the meeting room door. They won't be late again.

WHO'S THAT GUY IN THE CAN-CAN DRESS?

Don't knock having a little fun. It may the perfect prescription for boosting productivity. Emma Lou Brent, CEO at Phelps County Bank in Rolla, Missouri, says workers' high level of commitment at Phelps had caused stress, reports *Business Ethics*. When bank employees stopped having fun, productivity declined. But now the bank allows time for fun. Recently, male employees danced the can-can — in appropriate costumes — at a staff meeting.

Brent credits the initiatives with helping the bank reduce overhead by 3 percent and increase net income by 32 percent. But the fun isn't forced: No one is pressured to take part in any activity.

BANISH THOSE NEGATIVE THOUGHTS

The average person has more than 200 negative thoughts a day — that's the norm, according to *Strictly Business* magazine. If you're depressed, you could average 600 negative thoughts a day. The good news is that you can reduce the number of negative thoughts, including worries, anxieties, jealousies, and insecurities. Here's how:

1. When you begin having a negative thought, stay quiet for a few seconds. Talking tends to intensify the negative feelings associated with that thought.

2. Take five slow, deep breaths to lower your anxiety level. Visualize a relaxing scene such as walking on a beach at sunrise.

Learn to banish negative thoughts. You'll eventually find that fewer of them surface.

SPINNING YOUR WHEELS?

Changing priorities and a fast pace are becoming a way in life in business and industry today. Despite the hectic pace, however, you can put some direction into your life. Here are some tips:

- **Let your goals set your path.** What are your departmental goals for safety, quality, productivity, and customer service? Find out and tack them up where you can see them. They are your guideposts.

- **List your day's activities.** Initially, make the list a "wish list." Put down everything you wish you could do, if only you had the time.

- **Prioritize the list.** Label tasks as "important/urgent," "less important/urgent," or "less important/less urgent." Activities that directly help you accomplish your goals are those you should consider important. And remember that sometimes urgent activities have to take precedence over important ones. But items that have little importance to your goals, as well as little urgency, should take least priority. Consider if they have to be done at all.

- **Start with your top-priority items.** Treat new jobs that come up as items for your list: Postpone them if they fall into the lower ranks.

- **Decide what you can delegate.** Best candidates for delegation — tasks that someone else has the skills and knowledge to do. And remember that some tasks you simply cannot delegate.

- **Be practical about how you handle jobs.** For example, make a telephone call instead of writing a memo. Or, instead of composing a letter to reply to one you received, jot your answer or comments on the original letter and send it off.

- **Do first things first.** You might be tempted to do things you like first, Stick to your priority list; try to reduce the number of routine jobs you attend to; and increase the number of tough tasks you handle.

QUICK TIPS

- **Stop clock-watching.** When a project is important to complete, but not urgent, hide the clock and/or your wristwatch. This allows you to harness your internal rhythms and energy flow, says time management expert Jeff Davidson. Freed from the clock, you can engage fully in the task at hand.

- **Stretch yourself.** Athletes improve their techniques by increasing the level of difficulty. You too can work on your quality by constantly stretching yourself, taking risks, and trying new approaches. Only then can you grow.

- **Say it right.** Whenever you're given someone's business card, ask for the correct pronunciation of the individual's name and even the name of the organization. Then write them on the back of the card for handy reference.

- **Control Clutter.** Dianna Booher, author of *Clean Up Your Act!* (Warner Books), says that you can control desk clutter by placing a "destruction date" on each piece of paper that comes in. Example: "D-12-30-96."

- **Color code your to-do list.** You can quickly refocus on top-priority tasks if you color-code your daily to-do list. Use bright-colored markers for priority projects and muted colors for less important tasks.

- **Record your lessons.** In your next monthly activities report, include at least one item you have learned during the last 30 days. Committing to paper what you have learned, says Professor Jean Olthoff of Northern Illinois University, makes you more aware of applying learning to the job.

- **Spend time on timesavers.** Spending a few minutes on certain activities can save you hours in the long run. The activities: verifying information; keeping coworkers informed; rechecking your work; and asking for feedback from your boss.

ROAD LESS TRAVELED LEADS TO REWARDING DESTINATIONS

"I'm always impressed with a particular teammate. He always has a new idea, a different way of looking at old problems. My boss says this type of 'thinking out of the box' is a good way to promote Quality. How can I be more like my teammate?"

— P.W., San Jose, California

One of the best-kept secrets about creative thinking is that it does not come naturally for everyone. Many of the most creative individuals have learned *how* to think out of the box. They've learned that certain actions and behaviors will help trick their minds into new ways of thinking. It's a skill we can all develop to one degree or another. See how successful you are at reengineering your thinking. Write Yes or No after each question, then score yourself below.

1. Do you take the initiative to work on projects with someone with whom you've never worked before? _____

2. Have you ever volunteered for a task that "scares" you because you thought it was beyond you or too risky and challenging? _____

3. Have you tried learning a completely new skill? _____

4. Do you take part in brainstorming sessions where the floor is open to even the most "far out" solution to a problem? _____

5. Do you vary your schedule or take a different route to work to help start your day with a fresh new perspective? _____

6. Do you listen to the ideas and opinions of coworkers and appreciate the depth of their knowledge? _____

7. Are you always on the lookout for ways to cut costs and reduce errors? _____

8. Do you prioritize your tasks to focus on the most urgent but still leave time to pursue new ideas? _____

9. Do you use your weekends and vacation times as
periods to recharge your batteries and gain a fresh
perspective on how you do things? _____

10. Do you constantly reevaluate your strategies to
assure that you never stray too far off track? _____

YOUR CREATIVE QUOTIENT: Hopefully, you answered each
question Yes. That would indicate you already are very successful at getting into a more creative mindset. Seven or eight is
average. Look at those questions you responded No to, and
incorporate the behavior into your daily routine. You'll see a rise
in your creativity quotient.

YOUR QUALITY TAKE-AWAY

The Fourth Simple Thing You Can Do for
Your Company and Your Career:
Reengineer Your Thinking

Although many managers fear change, organizations depend on the infusion of new ideas and points of view to reach their quality objectives, particularly in terms of continuous improvement. Organizations need to teach leaders and managers to value thinking that is "out of the box." They need to stop assuming technology is the answer to every problem and seek innovative cost-saving ideas and solutions to other problems. *There may be barriers to the flow of creativity and innovation in the workplace, but the most important obstacle to overcome is the barrier within yourself.*

What *You* Can Do

- You need to be able to adapt to the ever-changing business climate so you can benefit from the career opportunities that will present themselves.

- Techniques like "flow" can help put you in a creative mindset.

- Look to the experience of others for lessons you can use in your life and career.

- Find ways to prioritize your time and to allot time to concentrate without interruptions. Seek more efficient ways for performing your duties.

- "Flip-flop" ideas to see problems in a new way; for example, by asking yourself how to *not* make customers happy, you may find yourself uncovering new and better ways to serve them better.

An innovative and creative outlook is valuable in your job today and in your future. Don't rest on your laurels — stretch yourself!

CHAPTER FIVE

BELIEVE IN YOUR OWN QUALITY

"The new truth is radically different. Quality is a very personal obligation. If you can't talk about quality in the first person. ... then you have not moved to the level of involvement that is absolutely essential. This is the most useful thing I can say. You must be a believer that quality is a very personal responsibility."
— BOB GALVIN, CHAIRMAN OF THE EXECUTIVE COMMITTEE, MOTOROLA, INC.

INTRODUCTION

If you've been at your job for many years, you probably have a routine that works well for you. It's unlikely that you often question just what you do or how you do it. On the other hand, if you're new at your job, you undoubtedly focus on learning the ropes. You ask questions about whom to see for information and materials, time schedules, and other mechanics of performing well in your new position.

In either case, think about how you would answer this question: "Do you *believe* in what you do?" Even if you don't know the answer, the people with whom you interact each day probably do. Consider these examples:

- When you provide superior service to either internal or external customers, you demonstrate that you believe in what you do on the job.

- When you deliver messages to coworkers promptly and accurately, you show that you believe in what you do.

- When you're available to help out and come through in emergencies, you demonstrate to management and your colleagues that you believe in what you do.

- When you talk enthusiastically and positively about your job with friends and family, you show a belief in what you do.

How can you strengthen or maintain a powerful belief in yourself and the importance of your day-to-day responsibilities at work? There are several ways that will fit easily into your routine, no matter how long it's been in place or how comfortable you feel with it.

1. Service counts. The next time you face a difficult customer, remind yourself that you perform a valuable service for your company. For the duration of the time with the customer (whether on the phone or face-to-face), you are the company. All of your coworkers are depending on you.

2. Satisfy the customer. A current or potential sale may be riding on it. Instead of thinking about how to "get rid of" the person as quickly as possible, summon up all the skills you have to bring about a satisfactory conclusion.

3. Stress quality. When you've got work backed up and waiting for attention, resist the initial impulse to hurry through each task. Each needs your undivided time and attention. If you cannot solve a particular problem yourself, seek help. Don't just pass it on to someone else.

4. Watch what you say. When speaking with people outside the company, you never know who is (or could be) a potential customer. Even if you're frustrated over a work-related matter, temper your remarks.

5. Support colleagues. Do your part to promote team spirit and to achieve common goals. Give ideas a fair hearing before dismissing them. Accentuate the positive aspects of work, rather than joining in when others complain.

6. Enjoy your successes. Sure, humility is an asset — but that doesn't mean you cannot luxuriate in some personal satisfaction when you've scored a professional victory. You earned some self-congratulations, so enjoy them. You'll confirm the belief that what you do is important, worthwhile, and gratifying. It's a belief that can make all the difference.

The ideas that follow can show you more ways to take control of your position and your career by believing in your own quality.

WRITE A QUALITY DEFINITION YOU CAN BELIEVE IN

Your organization wants to select a specific definition of quality for everyone to adhere to. With so many experts in the quality field, whose interrelation should you adopt?

Instead of relying on the experts, why not develop a definition that works for you? You and your coworkers can create a definition tailored to your organizational needs. That will result in quality that you can believe in.

Start by polling team members informally on what quality means to them. Ask them not to worry about finding the right words, but to speak from their hearts. Then, create a questionnaire based on what you've learned from talking to coworkers, and pool the results.

You can still learn a lot by reading what the experts have to say about quality. But, your definition will mean much more — and get more support — if you and your teammates have a hand in creating it.

GETTING INTO A QUALITY STATE OF MIND

Quality isn't solely a product of specific actions; it's also a product of state of mind. Therefore, reengineering your attitude is the key to improving work practices and results. That "quality mentality" is rooted in the knowledge that everything can be improved. Consider some of the following "rules" of quality thinking to put you in the right frame of mind:

1. There's no such thing as perfection. A product or service can always be improved. Even when one feature has been optimized, others can be enhanced. And when every feature of your product or service is sound, you might still be able to add new features. Think of it as a challenge to your imagination.

2. What's adequate today may not be tomorrow. Change never ceases. Last year's terrific innovation may be obsolete this year. So, even if you think you've reached the top in your field or product line, someone will come around tomorrow to redefine what "the top" is.

3. Change isn't always good. Looking for opportunities to make improvements is not the same as looking to change things. Rash changes — even when they seem to be good ideas — sometimes fall flat. Think in terms of the reason for a change.

4. Satisfaction is trouble. There's truth to the familiar saying: "That which ceases to grow begins to die." You'll need to sustain your hunger for improvement just to keep up with the demands of a world that has grown accustomed to constant improvements.

5. Seek out other people's opinions. You can't think of everything alone. Other people — even those who aren't experts — may have special ideas or insights of their own. So ask for coworkers' advice, and be prepared to act on it.

6. What seems logical and what works are two different things. Experience proves that, for every theory that works, 99 others don't. Good ideas deserve to be tested. By the same token, they must be tested before they should be accepted.

7. Consider the possibility that each new idea might create new problems. Keep in mind, therefore, that each attempt to improve one item might affect other elements. So watch out for potential repercussions from each new quality improvement you make. Also, check your finished product against a comprehensive list of quality objectives.

8. Quality is as quality does. Don't be presumptuous about quality. Changes for the better are not based on anyone's opinion, but on the evidence of absolute improvement and the favorable opinions of the buyers. So keep your eyes open.

QUALITY IS YOUR RESPONSE-ABILITY

"Responsibility is a unique concept," the late Admiral Hyman Rickover has been quoted as saying. "It can only reside and inhere in a single individual. You may share it with others, but your portion is not diminished. You may delegate it, but it is still with you. You may disclaim it, but you cannot divest yourself of it."

Anyone working for a quality-conscious organization also needs "response-ability." That's the skill that allows you to meet a job challenge in a responsible manner.

The term was coined by G. Michael Durst, Ph.D., president of Training Systems, Inc., in Evanston, Illinois. In family life, Durst maintains, there's no such thing as a "50-50 marriage." Each partner is 100 percent responsible for making the union work. Similarly, if a teacher's class is bored, it's because the teacher has failed to respond to the students' needs.

The same principle applies to the workplace. Durst explains: "The truth is simple. Whether we like it or not, we are responsible for everything in our experience. Liking or not liking a situation are only evaluations. Upon reflection, people typically report that what they thought to be negative was the perfect experience for them." For example, if you say, "They did it to me," you're acting as though you had no choice. Your response-ability level is zero. But, if you admit that you did something to yourself, that's an expression of total choice. You have a response-ability rating of 100 percent.

"In a quality team situation," Durst points out, "each member of the team is 100 percent responsible for the team's success. And, when you have that total commitment, you can ignite a spark in every team member."

Try to measure your own response-ability level. After each event that occurs at work to day, answer these questions:

- Did this event or a similar one ever take place before? Is there a pattern?

- What does the pattern have to do with your attitudes and behavior?

- Are you actually setting up the situation?

- If the event was negative, what can you do to avoid repeat occurrences?

- Whose responsibility is it to react in a positive manner, learn from the experience, and change negative patterns?

Says Durst: "Notice that it *all* comes back to *you*. In fact, response-ability begins and ends with you. Once you become aware of what makes life more satisfying and productive, that very wisdom will create a more quality-conscious style. The more successful you are as a person, the more successful you will become as a quality team player. Your work style directly reflects YOU."

FIVE LEADERSHIP SKILLS

When a quest for quality is involved, there only are leaders and no followers. And the leaders are you and everyone in your department, performing in ways that inspire others to excel. If you and your teammates can master certain skills, you will be on your way toward achieving the quality you seek. *Sourcebook* lists the following five basic leadership skills:

1. Communicating. Through actions and words, you and your coworkers can help build a better product or perform a superior service. You can start by talking matters out clearly. Don't think in "I" and "me" terms. Instead, make your points through "we" and "us" references. Get some of your ideas across through body language: smile, extend your arms to indicate an open stance. *Sourcebook* points out: "It's important to listen well, too. When someone has an idea, give him or her your undivided attention. Nothing alienates people faster than meeting a preoccupied gaze."

2. Motivating. The search for quality entails a common vision. You'll find that true motivation comes from challenges that are shared by everyone on the team. If you're part of a quality team, rotate the challenging projects and the routine ones so that nobody is always stuck with housekeeping chores. It's also essential to anticipate problems that could damage group morale. By thinking and planning ahead, you'll meet your current quality goals much more quickly.

3. Team building. Even if you and your associates haven't been organized into a formal quality work group, instill in yourself as well as in others a strong sense of teamwork. Each team member has a special talent. Working together, you can capitalize on each other's individual expertise. Acknowledge that every contribution has equal value. Also, think of ways to save your employer money or improve a product or service, and ensure that management learns where the idea came from.

4. Information gathering. Put your own resources to work through frequent fact-finding missions. Learn what you can by speaking with people in other departments and outside organizations. Share what you've learned with your coworkers at periodic meetings. Draw on their knowledge. If an idea shows the way to the successful conclusion of a quality project, give credit where it's due. *Sourcebook* adds: "Develop a sensitivity to others' ideas and learn how to apply them in your department. Meet with people from other groups and ask questions."

5. Gatekeeping. This calls for the combined skills of a salesperson and a diplomat. As gatekeepers, you and your associates must control the flow of ideas and information within and outside your department. If important quality-related decisions are initiated elsewhere, accept them and build on them. Similarly, if a workable idea comes from within your group, pass it on to your supervisor.

SUCCESS AS A LEADER?
FIRST BE A GOOD FOLLOWER

So many training programs focus on the concept of effective leadership — and so much has been written about today's outstanding leaders — that most of us have a relatively clear notion of what the characteristics of dynamic leaders are. For example, we know that a leader is someone who creates a vision, inspires others to commit to that vision, and develops strategies to move people toward it.

Many think of the typical leader as something of a hero, off by him- or herself, boldly blazing trails, making it possible for others to continue forward. What we often fail to notice is that most leaders are only as effective as the people who follow them and support their initiatives.

But what do we actually know about the leader's followers? Traditionally, the word "follower" has had a largely negative connotation. We tend to think of sheep, blindly and passively led, while offering nothing constructive in the process. But, that's nothing short of a gross misconception. As Robert Kelley, business professor at Pittsburgh's Carnegie Mellon University, states, "We make the assumption that leaders are effective and give them all this training. We assume that followers are ineffective, yet we don't train them. People are not born with either ability."

Kelley also observes that ... most of us are more often followers than leaders. Even when we have subordinates, we still have bosses. For every committee we chair, we sit as a member on others. ... In fact, it may be that learning to be a follower is at the very heart of leadership. For example, even some politicians have to follow the wishes of his or her constituency.

Since it's been said that the best leaders are also the best followers, it can be helpful to recognize what it takes to be an effective follower. Stephen Lunding, professor at Metropolitan

State University in Minneapolis, and Lynne Lancaster, a St. Paul, Minnesota, consultant, have observed that effective followers possess these characteristics:

- They have personal integrity that demands both loyalty to the organization and willingness to act according to their beliefs.

- They "own the territory," meaning they understand the organization and their contributions to it.

- They are versatile, skillful, and flexible enough to adapt to a changing environment.

- They take responsibility for their own careers, their own actions, and their own development.

Leadership skills can be learned. Adept followers eventually grow into fine leaders. If you strive to be a leader in your career, you have the opportunity to learn what it takes to inspire a loyal following somewhere down the pike.

PERFORMANCE BOOSTERS
THAT GET NOTICED

Want management to sit up and take notice of your performance? Barry Eigen, in *How to Think Like a Boss and Get Ahead at Work* (Carol Publishing Group), suggests keeping these six guiding principles in mind:

1. Fix it before it leaks. When problems arise, look for solutions and take them to the boss. Keep quiet about complaints.

2. Remember that nobody's perfect. Not even you. Admit mistakes, shortcomings, and imperfections, rather than trying to deny them or cover them up. Employees who "never make mistakes" suggest that they are playing it so safe that they lack creativity and confidence.

3. Avoid the entitlement trap. Raises and promotions are earned by work performance beyond expectations. They are not automatically guaranteed.

4. Sell yourself. Find opportunities to outline skills and accomplishments. Express a willingness to take on more responsibility. Bosses are usually so busy that they may not notice every individual's strengths until someone else brings them to their attention.

5. Give yourself a chance. Trust yourself to grow into new assignments, even though you might worry at first how the extra load will ever get done. Don't wait for the "perfect moment" to seize an opportunity. That time may never come.

6. Make the right friends. Cultivate friendships with upbeat peers. And don't forget to strike up alliances with those on higher levels. Avoid complainers, naysayers, and nitpickers.

TIME FOR A WORKOUT

Athletes improve their technique by increasing their level of endurance, strength, or speed. Similarly, you can develop your career by stretching yourself, taking risks, and trying new things. Only then can you hope to improve and grow personally and professionally.

NO NEED FOR HEROICS!

If one person has to go above and beyond the call of duty to make quality work, then your quality system isn't working up to par. That's the assumption leaders of the Israeli army work under when they investigate acts of heroism.

Whenever an Israeli soldier earns a medal for valor, the

heroic efforts signal that something is askew, reports David Lloyd, consultant with Pittsburgh-based Development Dimensions International (DDI). Leaders attempt to find out how they can prevent the need for bravery and personal risk in the future.

The lesson: If you're having to perform heroics to get the job done, look at the system to see how to improve its efficiency.

Are You Tough Enough to Win the Quality Battle?

Like every other goal in life, the quest to attain high-quality performance doesn't come easily. It requires a fighting effort against odds that often look long. "Many of us dream of a fantasy world without problems," William Eddy writes in *Personal Selling Power.* "In reality, all of us will meet obstacles and have setbacks or misfortunes. No matter how well we plan and prepare for the future, problems will sometimes wear us down, drain vitality and enthusiasm, and make our goals seem out of reach. Discouragement is like quicksand. We must pull ourselves out quickly or sink even deeper."

Many people with good backgrounds and fine talents fail for just one reason. When they're hit the hardest, they don't have the ability to fight back. As you push toward your company and personal quality goals, Eddy offers six tactics you can employ to keep in top "fighting" form:

1. Keep busy. Whether you're at work or home, resist the temptation to do nothing but sit around. By being active, you'll stimulate energy and restore vitality. "A person creates upbeat feelings by energetic activities," Eddy points out. "Walk as if you had something urgent to do."

2. Think positively. Read biographies of people who over-came adversity and watch movies that have courage as a theme.

Associate with people who are well disciplined. "Avoid anyone who will pamper or hamper you," Eddy urges, "and don't listen to negative talk."

3. Remember past successes. When you feel discouraged, get a notebook and write down every past hardship you conquered. Go as far back as your childhood and recall how you felt when you overcame each obstacle.

4. Be grateful. "A despondent attitude can't coexist with a grateful attitude," Eddy asserts. "Eventually, one will destroy the other. Talk about everything likable that you see, hear, or read. And, spend at least 10 minutes before you go to sleep thinking of everything you have to be grateful for."

5. Correct your mistakes. We're all responsible for many of our problems. When troubles occur, take a careful look at all the factors that contribute to them. Evaluate your weaknesses and strengths. Most important, don't feel ashamed. None of us can become wise unless failure teaches us how to move ahead.

6. Maintain your integrity. "Adversity is a test of integrity," Eddy explains. "Learn to feel that you deserve the best. Do what's right and you'll feel right about yourself. Self-discipline requires that we push ourselves beyond what's comfortable. By trying hard enough, we can become tough enough to win."

WHAT'S YOUR E.Q.? (ETHICAL QUOTIENT)

Believing in your own quality requires that you have confidence in the day-to-day decisions you make in your job. Some of the toughest decisions you make involve a choice between right and wrong. How do you fare when ethical issues arise? Take this quiz and find out.

1. A supplier you do business with shows up one day with a gift for you: a four-head VCR with on-screen programming. What do you do?

a. Accept the gift and keep it at the office for everyone to use.

b. Say, "Throw in a tape of *Forrest Gump* and we're in business!"

c. Say, "Thanks, but no thanks."

2. Your boss asks you to record a phone conversation without the other person's knowledge. What do you do?

a. Say, "OK, but if we're caught, you have to take the responsibility."

b. Repeat the request. "Do I understand correctly that you're asking me to tape a phone conversation without the other person's knowledge?"

c. Go along. After all, she's your boss.

3. You hear a coworker tell an all-out lie to a customer. What should you do?

a. Ignore it; you'll be accused of eavesdropping.

b. Tell the coworker, "That's a good one. I'll have to use that one on my callers!"

c. Tell a supervisor what you heard.

ANSWERS

Judge your responses against what the experts say:

1. (c) Accepting notepads or a calendar from a printer who wants your business is one thing. But a VCR? No way. Do not accept the gift. "And if a supplier offers a gift that is out of line with professional standards, you should report it immediately to your supervisor so there is no doubt about your integrity," says Elena Jankowic, author of *Behave Yourself!* (Morrow).

2. (b) Repeating the request back (with a look of mild shock on your face) lets your boss know you know it's unethical. "And it gives him or her a chance to back out," says ethics expert Nan DeMars. "If he or she doesn't back out, you should refuse."

3. (c) Don't say anything to the coworker. But if you're sure that what you heard was an all-out lie, talk to your supervisor — in confidence. Tell what you heard. "After yourself, you have a duty to protect your company," says DeMars.

LEARN TO BE THE BEST

Norman Best worked as a laborer for 50 years. He began his formal education in the classroom, and completed it on the plant floor. Early in his career, he took night-college courses to learn new concepts and problem-solving ideas. He applied that education to his manufacturing career.

Best has experienced some of the best work practices, and survived some of the worst. He is a profound believer in team-work, continuous learning, and creative problem solving. He chronicles his observations and experiences in his book *Celebrations of Work* (University of Nebraska Press).

Best summarizes what he considers the most important lessons for surviving workplace changes and remaining a proud, knowledgeable, and contributing employee:

- **Take small steps.** Having worked for many different plants and experienced many job changes, Best found the best way to acclimate to change is to approach it one small step at a time. "You can start out small and increase your chance at succeeding at a task, or you can bite off more than you can chew and increase your risk of failure," says Best.

- **Keep on learning.** Take advantage of all training opportunities. It doesn't matter how long you've been doing the same job; you can always learn something new. "As a young man, I wanted to get into the machinist trade. I had a lot of informal experience and thought I knew everything," says Best. "When I finally got a job, I bragged about all my 'experience,' and soon found out that was my biggest mistake. My boss said, 'Well, son, that's a lot of experience you'll have to unlearn before you work here.' I had to relearn everything to do things the way the company wanted me to do them."

- **Be a team player.** You can either be a team member or you can be a team player. The difference lies in your level of participation. "I once supervised a team of workers with varying degrees of ability," Best explains. "The more experienced workers taught the others what they knew. Each member mastered the skills required of the whole team. Eventually, team members were able to rotate assignments so that no one member had to consistently do the more difficult work due to another's lack of ability."

- **Include your supervisor.** A common misconception among production workers is that the supervisor is their enemy — someone who watches over them and documents their mistakes. "I learned to always inform my supervisor of any new developments or problems," says Best. "Be fair with your supervisor and he will be fair with you. Make it easy for your supervisor to support you; keep him informed. If you don't keep him informed, you can't blame him for not supporting your efforts — he can't support what he doesn't know or doesn't understand."

DOWNSIZING IS TOUGH ON SURVIVORS, TOO

Few organizations today are safe from downsizing, whether it's due to reengineering, a merger, or a takeover by new management. Living through downsizing can be almost as rough on the survivors as it is on the victims. Even if you've managed to survive with your job intact, downsizing can be tough to take. Although more and more organizations are providing support for downsizing survivors, the onus is still basically on your own ability to cope. Here's how:

1. Maintain your standards. If you're feeling angry that coworkers and friends have been laid off, it may be tempting to give less than your all. But underneath it all, you know you're capable of more and will probably feel worse if you are not working up to your usual standards. What's more, reduced performance may even jeopardize your own job security. What's done is done, and you're not doing your company, yourself, or anyone else any good by caving in to the forces of mediocrity.

2. Keep your attitude under control. Everyone has to take hard knocks in life. What separates survivors from quitters is what they choose to do with the circumstances. No one expects you to think that everything is just wonderful. But, it serves no useful purpose to let your attitude deteriorate into anger, pessimism, hostility, and bitterness. Even if you don't always have control over the events around you, you should be in charge of how you react to those events.

3. Find ways to vent your frustrations. It's normal to feel a sense of loss, as well as worry and anger after your workplace is disrupted. Acknowledge that you're going through a tough time. You accomplish nothing if you bottle feelings up — only to explode at a colleague over nothing. If you need to talk, find someone you can trust outside the organization. Get things off your chest so you can work without harboring resentment.

4. Tend to your physical and emotional health. When under stress, it's important to take care of yourself in all respects. Make sure you eat well, get enough sleep and exercise, and devote time to leisure. This is not the time to miss work due to stress-induced illness.

5. Take rumors in stride. Some people enjoy playing the "let's trade horror stories" game to see who knows the scariest piece of news. These discussions only serve to escalate fears that the worst is yet to come. In your central job position, you may become the sounding board for frustrated coworkers. They may even come to you hoping to hear some confidential information. Keep focused on the known facts and give scant attention to everything else.

6. Initiate an employee-suggestion program. If you don't already have one, talk to the boss. To get started, investigate established programs in other companies to see how they operate. In the long run, a suggestion program gives employees a voice and reduces the feeling of powerlessness people typically feel during a downsizing.

It's easy to succumb to the discouragement that follows a company downsizing. Despite the uncertainty and discomfort, eventually things will settle down into a new pattern of normality. In the meantime, your survival depends not so much on what actually happens to you, but on your reactions to it.

STRESS ADDICTS CREATE CRISES, THEN RUSH TO THE RESCUE

Between work and home, most of us experience more stress than we know what to do with. We would welcome a little more calmness in our lives. But, some people thrive on a high-pressure, thrill-a-minute style of work that can bring most of us to nervous exhaustion.

They're the ones who welcome crises, trying to beat the clock by saving a project from disaster at the last possible moment. Their credo: "I work best under pressure." Some thrive on drama or the adrenaline surge created by urgency. Others like the notion of being a hero coming to the rescue. Yet others fear failure, so they put off tasks until they have no choice but to do them — and any mistakes can be blamed on the lack of time left to actually complete projects.

Often, however, these individuals can function only under

these extreme conditions. They might even manufacture urgency (through procrastination, for example), compelling coworkers to work under the same stressful circumstances.

Not only is this practice unfair to your coworkers, it's usually counterproductive as well — these stress "addicts" may leave nothing but mistakes, resentment, and pandemonium in their wake.

Those who hope to move ahead in their careers must be able to adopt a work style that uses time most effectively for everyone involved. Are you a stress addict? If you tend to welcome stressful work conditions that drive others crazy, perhaps you should consider a change to bring your addiction under control. Here are some suggestions to consider:

1. Identify the problem. Take a close look at how you typically work. Is the stress in your job due to external influences or created, to some extent, by you? Can this stress be avoided or reduced? Do you even want to change? There's little hope of change if you don't see the problem.

2. Ask coworkers for feedback. If you're still unsure, ask colleagues how your behavior affects them. Your coworkers may actually reinforce your stress habit. They might typically pick up the pieces, make excuses or rationalize your behavior, or suffer silently. Create an environment that encourages candid responses.

3. Discuss specific incidents. Look for patterns in your behavior. What could be done differently? Ask for constructive suggestions on how you could have operated differently. You might have to strike a deal with coworkers that you will avoid emergency requests; plan ahead on long-term tasks; or curb any procrastinating.

4. Keep your eyes and ears open. Look for the danger signals that you're lapsing into the crisis habit. Look at individual stress situations to determine the cause. Control what you can.

Encourage your colleagues to bring to your attention any warning signals as well.

Granted, stress is a part of almost every job. Most of us can manage it effectively — at least most of the time. But, creating a breakneck environment can prevent you from working at your best and being an effective team player. It can reduce coworker cooperation and thwart any plans for a move into a supervisory or management position. Those with less stress in their lives are happier as well as emotionally and physically healthier.

TAKING A BREAK IS OK

"In spite of their tremendous drive to excel and to achieve, successful people value nurturing relationships and leisure time. They understand that they are not simply machines that can put on high levels of energy and perform without refueling. They accept their need for nurturance and support. Successful people look forward to taking a break."

— DR. E. CAROL WEBSTER, *SUCCESS MANAGEMENT,*
PRIVILEGED COMMUNICATIONS, INC.

WANT QUALITY WORK RELATIONSHIPS?
THINK SMALL

Close ties with coworkers can improve work quality, a Purdue University study shows. Assistant professors Shelley M. MacDermid and Margaret L. Williams examined coworker relationships, working conditions, and family-work tensions among 60 mothers serving customers in large and small banks.

The researchers found that closeness among workers develops most easily in small workplaces. "Formal rules and layers of bureaucracy in large work settings may hinder the looseness that employees need to coordinate their own solutions," Odette Pollar notes in *Organizing Your Workspace* (Crisp Publications).

To foster close, productive relationships, employees need the following, say MacDermid and Williams: to treat people and be treated fairly; to communicate openly; to meet in groups; to work in open areas without physical obstructions; and to receive awards that aren't based on competition.

QUICK TIPS

- **Time shift tip.** If your work shift changes time, requiring that you work at night and sleep during the day, it's important that you still get eight hours of sleep. To help, trick your body into thinking it's night by sleeping in a room with no windows or buying room-darkening shades to give the illusion of night. Then dream away.

- **Blame no one but yourself.** The word *blame* contains the word *lame*, notes Arthur Freeman, author of *The 10 Dumbest Mistakes Smart People Make* (HarperCollins). Blaming others, regardless of who is at fault, does nothing to solve problems. When possible, take the initiative to solve problems on your own.

- **Bench yourself.** A good place to begin benchmarking is with yourself, suggests *Business Ethics.* Analyze what you do successfully in your own company, and then look for ways you can adapt your own best practices to other areas of your company.

- **Build trust.** If you work closely with your colleagues, it's vital that you treat them in terms of skill, honesty, and reliability — and that they trust you. Mutual trust is a critical element in good communication, cooperation, and coordinated service.

- **Keep track of going off-track.** Conclude your meetings faster by designating one person to track interruptions. You may be surprised by how often you go off-track.

- **Generate interest in your ideas.** When you want to pass ideas on to your team leader or supervisor, *Office Proficiency* suggests, try this: "I've got some ideas you'll find interesting. Is this a good time to talk?" A "yes" response guarantees his or her full attention.

- **Pick out the positive.** Don't get sucked into office gripe sessions. Instead, take an entire day and promise yourself to say only positive things. Once you start looking at the bright side in every situation, you'll wonder what you were doing in the dark. Make optimism a habit.

GAIN CONTROL OF YOUR TIME

"If there's any single obstacle that keeps me from attaining my personal quality goals, it's the fact that I don't always know the best way to prioritize my time. When the day is complete, I'll often find that I never made it to some of the most important work I needed to complete."

— **T. S. B., Cleveland, Ohio**

There are so many demands made on us today, it's often difficult to get everything done. But do you know what's most important to do now and which things can be put off until later? Too many of us react to that issue by doing the easiest or fastest task, which may not be the most important. Or, we respond by putting everything off.

Test how you would react by prioritizing the following list of things you need to take care of when you walk into work tomorrow. Number them in order of importance, labeling the most important No. 1, and so on.

_____Returning calls to customers

_____Seeing your boss about a problem

_____Calling a prospective customer

_____Completing preliminary work for the day (arranging tools, checking schedules, etc.)

_____Returning a call to a colleague

_____Starting a two-week project

_____Checking your voice mail, e-mail, and in-box

_____Tapping in to the office grapevine

_____Talking with colleagues who dealt with your customers while you were away

_____Getting briefed about new policies or products

RATE YOUR PRIORITIES: There isn't one best way to handle the above 10 tasks, since it would depend on your individual circumstances. However, the following list prescribes a sensible course of action:

No. 1 — Seeing your boss about a problem should be your first order of business. The nature of the problem may dictate how you arrange the rest of your tasks.

No. 2 — Getting yourself set up for the day.

No. 3 — Checking your incoming messages. Chances are your messages will provide you with additional items to add to your list.

No. 4 — Returning calls to customers should be in your top five.

No. 5 — Calling a prospective customer should probably come next.

No. 6 — Talking with colleagues who dealt with your customers while you were away.

No. 7 — Finding out about new policies or products.

No. 8 — Returning a call to a colleague.

No. 9 — Starting a two-week project.

No. 10 — Tapping in to the office grapevine, where you'll hear about the events you missed.

YOUR QUALITY TAKE-AWAY

The Fifth Simple Thing You Can Do for
Your Company and Your Career:

Believe in Your Own Quality

Quality is like an upside-down pyramid. At the top are the concepts and processes that management undertakes to implement a quality program. At the bottom is you — the individual who holds up the rest of the pyramid with your personal commitment to making quality succeed.

What *You* Can Do

- Show that you believe in your own quality by taking personal responsibility for everything you do.

- Be aware that the service you provide to internal and external customers ... the enthusiasm you show for your work ... the commitment you show to everything you do — these all convey that you know the vital role you carry out in making quality succeed.

- Control stress so you feel more in control of your life.

- Maintain your integrity so you'll be assured of the respect of your teammates.

- Challenge complacency, both personally and in your work.

Remember that you have to sustain a hunger for improvement just to keep up with the demands of a world that has grown accustomed to constant improvements and change.

CHAPTER SIX

Sign Your Work

"Every job is a self-portrait of the person who did it.
Autograph your work with excellence."
— **Commitment to Quality,**
Great Quotations, Inc.

INTRODUCTION

"My job is a challenge to my personal discipline, to my integrity. I put my spirit, my soul into this product. If you do it perfectly every time, you are teaching yourself excellence." These are not the words of a corporate executive or a company owner. Nor are they taken from an organization's mission statement. They were spoken by a woman named Hwang, who works for the Samsung Corporation in Korea. She does not have a high-ranking position in the company. Her job is to attach serial-number plates and brand-name labels to Samsung microwave ovens. As her words indicate, Hwang does not only put her company's "signature" on each product. She puts her *personal signature* on her work. That's evident by the quality she puts in every aspect of her work.

Judith Bardwick, author of *Danger in the Comfort Zone* (AMACOM), describes Hwang's job this way: "She attaches about 1,200 labels a day. Six days a week, hour after hour, she does the same, simple thing. Even after the inspector has double-checked her work, she herself checks it one more time. It wasn't long ago that Korea was poor. It's not poor anymore. Hwang believes she is contributing to something very important — to Korea itself. "

What's the point of Bardwick's example? Every job and task in every organization is significant. Your work is important; it is a critical part of a big picture. When you strive for excellence in even the smallest things you do each day, you do your part to make your company better. When you put your personal signature behind everything you do, you are, in effect, giving your work your personal guarantee. You show you stand behind your work. This sense of commitment determines, more than anything else, how people perceive your personal quality.

But your commitment must extend beyond yourself. Just as the quality of your organization is determined in part by the level of your personal quality, so is your quality affected by the level of other people's quality. And you contribute directly to raising the quality level of those around you by demanding a high level of quality from others as well as yourself.

Don't allow other people to deliver inferior quality. Don't accept quality that does not live up to expectations. If you are not satisfied with the quality of someone else's work, you have a responsibility to say so. Demanding quality is just as important as delivering it. Just ask Hwang.

In what other ways can you put your personal signature on your work? The following suggestions can show you.

Guidelines Important to Peer Appraisals

Expecting quality from your coworkers is an important part of your personal quality initiative, so your company is launching a new peer performance appraisal system. You're on the committee that is developing guidelines for this system and don't know what elements of job performance you should be addressing.

Peer appraisal systems can have an advantage over traditional methods of review. Employees who work side by side often have a better understanding of each other's job functions than a "hands-off " boss would.

However, without some guidance, employees faced with reviewing their coworkers for the first time can find the task daunting. Either they'll "under-analyze" and say the employee does everything "fine," or they'll "over-criticize" and pick their peer apart. A clear set of job elements on which to rate the employee can help shape your new process. Here are some suggested traits to critique:

- **Dependability and reliability.** Does the employee get work done when it was promised in the condition it was promised? Such measurements as tardiness, absenteeism, and missed deadlines are useful in reviewing these traits.

- **Problem-solving skills.** A good employee is one who can not only identify problems and weaknesses, but can work out a way to address them. Does the employee complain about inefficient systems and procedures, or does he or she do something to fix them?

- **Commitment to customer service.** This skill is important whether you are actually answering customer service phone lines or working on the shop floor. Does the employee think of the customer as someone far removed from his or her job? Or does your coworker keep the customer's needs in mind during any task?

- **Teamwork skills.** No employee can afford to be a "loner" today. A sense of team play should exist throughout your workplace. Is the employee a supporter of working together, or would he or she prefer to be left alone?

- **Quality commitment.** How important is quality to this employee, as evidenced by the work produced and the attitude expressed? Every employee should be reviewed on his or her level of support of and involvement in quality initiatives.

Your list will include additional review points, based on what your organization does. Basic job skills haven't been included in this list because it should be assumed that every employee at your company has those basic skills, or he or she wouldn't be a member of the workforce. If those skills aren't present, management should address the issue.

PEER REVIEW PUTS TEAM'S STAMP OF QUALITY ON EVERY JOB

Like many companies, United Technologies Microelectronics Center in Colorado Springs, Colorado, recently underwent downsizing.

To enable fewer employees to complete more work, the semi-conductor designer and manufacturer formed teams, which meant that employees became acutely aware of their teammates' work activities. It seemed logical, then, that the company decided to implement a peer review system — a decision that most employees welcomed, according to team leader, Duke Shearer.

Quality is everyone's business. When you review your peers, you demonstrate that you expect quality from your teammates — the same quality they can expect from you. "Employees are closer to each other's performance than their supervisor," notes Shearer. "Their thinking was: 'If we're going to work as a team, I want something to say about the performance of other employees.'"

On Shearer's team of 14 employees, each member writes his or her own review, plus those of at least four peers. Shearer also completes a review of each team member. To monitor the whole team, members initiated a system of "speeding tickets." "Members continually review each other's work. Whenever anyone catches a mistake — no matter how small — they write it down like a ticket," explains Shearer. The employee who commits the infraction receives a copy of the ticket, while the original is placed in a box. The tickets are reviewed monthly by the entire team. "It's all done in good nature and allows employees to critique one another on an ongoing basis," says Shearer. "It makes everyone sharper."

Should peer review be introduced by your company, says Shearer, approach it fairly, honestly, and objectively. He offers two warnings:

1. Don't be an easy grader. You don't want to say, "Since we're going to review each other, let's make everyone look good." In the long run, you might prevent a coworker from obtaining the help he or she needs to address a particular job performance problem.

2. Don't use peer review as a weapon. "The process should not be used as a tool of revenge or spite," says Shearer. Remember that if you give a peer an unfairly negative review, he or she can do the same to you.

So, make your review neither too nice nor too harsh, and your team will get the constructive feedback it needs to keep moving forward.

WOULD YOU PASS THE 'BONE MARROW' TEST?

If you thought your test-taking days were long over, think again. Each day, your coworkers, your customers, and your supervisors all quietly measure you and your skills. They test to see how well you solve quality problems, if you know how to listen effectively, if you are able to set reasonable goals, and if you can carry out plans of action.

People are most interested in one particular area — your "bone marrow," claims John P. Schuster, author of *Hum-Drum to Hot-Diggity: Creating Everyday Greatness in the World of Work* (Steadfast Publishers).

"They are going to see what you're really made of — do you have bone-marrow, deep-down integrity? Do you walk your talk? Do you do what you say you are going to do? Do you earn their trust?" asks Schuster.

Are you comfortable with all that scrutiny directed at you? If not, you need to ask yourself why. What aren't you doing that you should?

Integrity is your most important property, says Schuster And people earn their reputations for integrity through little things they do every day. "It is often the small, but timely, gesture of thanks, the thoughtfulness of follow-through and getting back to someone, or sticking to a principle, even in a relatively unimportant matter, that builds your character and reputation," says Schuster.

Unfortunately, he says, there are some undisciplined people who lack integrity. "These are the people who tell their peers one thing and then do another. They are the ones who pad expense reports, take gifts that are too generous from vendors, and otherwise stay slightly sleazy," says Schuster.

"Good ethics are good business, and integrity, therefore, is your most important asset," emphasizes Schuster. "If you fail someday, but you still have your integrity, then you can pick yourself up and get on with it. But if you fail and do not keep your integrity, then you have got some major rebuilding to do."

And don't worry about making mistakes, he advises. "Get in there and make some decisions and learn from the wrong ones as much as from the right ones. Be sure to be a big enough person to admit that you're learning and that you've made some bad judgments.

"When you do that, you give others permission to admit their mistakes and to learn accordingly. That's important because only organizations with people who are learning are going to be able to survive and prosper into the future," says Schuster.

Back Up Your Work
with Personal Guarantees

One way to sign your work is to provide your customers with your personal guarantee. Your "warranty" shows that you have integrity and faith in the services you offer. Providing "free" warranty work can earn your organization a priceless commodity — customer loyalty.

Author Michael LeBoeuf relates how a California building contractor is doing so in *Fast Forward: How to Win More Business in a Lot Less Time* (Berkley). John Gremer installs residential building products such as roofs, gutters, ceiling fans, and insulation. The San Jose entrepreneur also does plumbing, electrical, heating, and air-conditioning repairs.

Under California law, contractors must furnish a one-year labor warranty for all building work. But Gremer adds a special touch to this service that the law doesn't require. After 11 months, he calls each customer and delivers this message: "We value your business, and your warranty expires next month. Is there any work you need done while it's still under warranty?"

Gremer's other goodwill gambit involves his $50-an-hour labor charge for repair work. If a call is completed in 40 minutes, the technician tells the home owner that he or she still has 20 minutes of service coming and volunteers to do other repairs. After Gremer introduced that policy, business went up by 30 percent.

Don't falsely assume that providing "free" service means that you can give customers what they pay for — nothing. Instead, use it as an opportunity to show your customers that your quality is priceless.

YOUR ROLE IN QUALITY

Business basic: If you make a product or provide a service that doesn't measure up to customers' expectations, a competitor will. For companies, that means lost business; for employees, it could mean lost jobs. This hard fact makes quality one of the key issues in today's global marketplace. And quality means taking the initiative to do your job right. Period. Whether you make telephone cords or nuclear submarines, whatever leaves your area must not only conform to specifications, it must also be the best you are capable of producing.

We all know people who take the easy way out and "pass the buck" for poor performance on to others. They blame bad materials, broken machines, accidents, and standards that are too high — or too low. Whatever the excuse, they fail to take responsibility for what they produce. As a result, their work is low quality, which hurts team productivity as well as company profitability.

To keep from passing the buck, take responsibility for every piece of work you produce. If you have a problem with maintaining the quality level, talk to a supervisor and find out where the problem lies. If it's machines or office equipment, fix them. And if the problem is with you, get "fixed" yourself by reviewing your current skills or retraining to build new ones.

With change being the norm in business today, it's smart to constantly seek ways to improve and become a valuable contributor. Sometimes that means going back to basics and brushing up on reading and math skills. Many companies now offer programs to allow employees to learn new skills. At General Electric, for example, 11,000 of 38,000 workers have taken a company-sponsored, two-day course in problem solving. Since jobs will become more complex, workers who stay abreast of new technology and procedures will have the best chance of staying competitive.

Teams that are motivated and take charge of their own operations can work miracles. At Levi Strauss' plant in Roswell, New Mexico, a self-managed team of 13 workers did the work of 25 and turned out six times the product. They each learned how to do three jobs and studied ways to reduce labor costs and make a work area more efficient. Instead of passing the buck, the Levi team found ways to meet problems head-on and create solutions that made them more productive.

Quality and productivity are dependent on everyone in the chain doing the best job possible. You, too, can make that commitment.

THE NINE C'S IN QUALITY

You'll improve your productivity and work standards if you keep in mind the nine C's that comprise on-the-job quality.

Writing in *Personnel Journal*, Walter B. Newsom, Ph.D., tells managers how to motivate employees. Adapting his theories to a quality-team setting, these are the C's that will bring out your best:

1. Capability. Do you have the capability to perform your job well? If you don't, you may need more training at work or study at home. New hires may not have sufficient capability because they lack both training and experience. Help them to prove that they can contribute.

2. Confidence. Says Newsom: "Without confidence, capability is limited. As a person becomes more capable, his or her confidence level should grow." However, that's not always the case. Your leader may assume that you can perform well, but perhaps you don't feel you're ready to go it alone. In time, you will.

3. Challenge. "Some employees literally sleep on the job," Newsom declares. "This is a major problem with work that's routine and presents no challenge. Quality suffers severely."

This is also true when employees are given difficult tasks without proper training. "The best results are obtained when people are stretched and believe that, with effort, they can perform the task," says Newsom.

4. Criteria. Without proper measuring devices, you may not know whether you're performing up to expectations. If your leader and supervisor don't provide guidelines, ask for them. Further, define the roles that your novice teammates must play.

5. Credibility. You must deliver what you promise. Excuses won't compensate for failure in the eyes of your teammates and your employer.

6. Consistency. When the late Vince Lombardi was coach of the Green Bay Packers, team star Jerry Kramer said that Lombardi treated everyone the same — like dogs. That's not consistency, Newsom asserts. He explains: "Consistency means that all high performers are treated similarly and all low performers are treated alike. Each group, however, is treated differently."

7. Compensation. This consists of much more than pay. Job satisfaction is a principal element, as is the feeling of being part of a winning team. A good manager, Newsom says, will tell you that you've done well. As a team, you should also pat each other on the backs.

8. Cost. "Everything anyone or any organization does involves an opportunity cost," Newsom observes. "Something must be given up to gain something else." By taking on a difficult assignment, the immediate costs may be significant. But, the effort you expend now could result in a big payoff later.

9. Communication. Behavioral changes may be needed. Teammates who like to talk must learn to listen; quiet ones must be prodded to participate. Newsom remarks: "Communication is vital to understand the other eight C's. Together, the nine C's represent a powerful tool."

THE POWER OF POSITIVE ENERGY

It's so easy to look around and notice what's wrong. It takes practice to see what's right. Many of us have lived around negativity for years. We've become skilled at labeling what's wrong. . . . Negative thinking empowers the problem. Negative energy sabotages and destroys. It has a powerful life of its own.

So does positive energy. Each day, we can ask what's right, what's good — about our people, our life, our work, our day, our relationships, ourselves, our conduct.

Positive energy transforms. Choose positive energy.

— MELODY BEATTIE, *THE LANGUAGE OF LETTING GO,* (HARPER/HAZELDEN)

INTERNAL ADVERTISING PROMOTES UNDERSTANDING BETWEEN TEAMS

A little "internal advertising" can go a long way in maintaining cooperation and understanding between your team and other departments and teams. It's also a way for your team to sign its work and show others the quality they can expect from you.

"Internal advertising is letting people in other parts of the organization know what you can do," says Lawrence G. Hrebiniak, a professor of strategic management at the Wharton School, University of Pennsylvania. "It's giving notice of your capabilities and who does what, attaching names to certain processes and services."

To get your advertising campaign off to a good start, circulate a memo explaining your team's function and the individual responsibilities of each member. Then, list services your team can provide to other teams in your organization. This tactic will definitely gain your peers' interest. Then, consider jobs or projects on which you could use the expertise of other teams and enlist their help.

IN PRAISE OF PRAISE

In a quality environment, you should expect quality from others. But you should not take their efforts for granted. A good way to reinforce good work is to recognize it with a hearty compliment. The result will be increased harmony within a work group or between departments and more attention to getting other jobs done right.

Here are some tips for giving high-quality praise:

- **Be specific.** Say: "The three additional points you added to that report really explained a difficult concept well." Don't say: "Nice work!"

- **Be generous.** When you hear a compliment about a coworker who isn't present, find that coworker and share the praise with him or her.

- **Put it in writing.** To reinforce a verbal compliment, follow up with a memo and a copy to appropriate associates and superiors.

Pat on the Back Can Boost Productivity Fast

"If all of a sudden you found yourself facing someone with a sign around his neck that said, 'Make me feel important,' what would you do?" asks Lee Evans Knapp, president of Knapp Consultants, Inc., in Fort Meyers, Florida, in *Sam's Buy-Line*. "Could you do it? Would you do it?" he asks. "Every day, we face people who are wearing that invisible sign. Everyone wants to feel important, and we can help."

Making others feel important inspires teamwork and can increase productivity quickly in the short term. Here's how to do it:

1. Respond immediately. For example, if you're sitting when a new worker is introduced to your team, rise, step forward, smile, maintain eye contact, clearly state your name, shake hands, and repeat the other person's name. Your body language reveals your level of interest.

2. Ask questions. Learn about people and their interests. Questions that can't be answered simply yes or no encourage others to open up to you. If the person is someone you'll be working with often, you'll develop helpful insights to smooth your work relationship.

3. Listen. Really pay attention to what people say. In the workplace, listening can be twice as important as talking. Yet the art of listening isn't taught in schools. "Some people don't listen long enough to even hear your name. That says to me that the person doesn't really care about me," Knapp says.

4. Give praise. This is a powerful motivator. When you tell a teammate "Good job!" you've turned a work associate into a work friend.

BRING THE BEST
OUT OF THE WORST PEOPLE

Team members need to cooperate, but what happens if you "can't stand" one of your teammates? "Just as some people bring out the best and the worst in you, you can learn to bring out the best in other people even when they are at their worst," says Dr. Rick Kirschner, coauthor with Rick Brinkman of *Dealing With People You Can't Stand* (McGraw-Hill).

Kirschner describes difficult personalities and how to handle them:

- **The tank.** "When you show up on a tank's radar screen, he simply starts blasting away at you," says Kirschner. To deal with him, hold your ground, look him in the eye, and control your breathing. Calmly interrupt the barrage by repeating his name. Then, say something like:

  "I know that you are tired of being slowed down by bureaucracy, but this is not the time to look at how the organization functions. Right now, we're looking at this team project. When we're done with this, let's talk."

- **The know-it-all.** This person does know a lot. She just doesn't think that other people do. "Slip in new ideas under her radar before she gets defensive," says Kirschner. For example, say: "What do you think would happen if we did this? I'd like your opinion."

- **The sniper.** The sniper tries to undermine your sense of control by finding out what causes you to react and then firing this at you when you're vulnerable. The secret is to make his covert operation overt. Stop what you're doing when he attacks. Look right at him and repeat whatever he said: "I heard you say that you think I am incompetent. What does this have to do with our project?" The sniper either has to keep quiet or answer you, says Kirschner. "Immediately after your meeting, however, meet with the person and ask for an explanation."

- **The "yes-person."** She says "yes" readily, then breaks her promise. Maybe she doesn't get the work done because she is disorganized. Or maybe she is afraid to say "no." Whatever the reason, make it safe for the yes-person to talk freely. For example, say: "I'm sure you meant to get the project done by 2 p.m., but it's late. What happened?" Her response might be: "I couldn't get to it because the phones kept ringing." Recognize her response for what it is: the possible cause of the problem. "Turn the situation into a learning moment by teaching the yes-person what to do," says Kirschner.

Relationships don't happen to you. They happen *through* you. Become a positive filter to help even the worst people be at their best.

EVERY ETHICAL CHOICE
CARRIES YOUR SIGNATURE

Just about everyone confronts ethical dilemmas in the workplace at some time. You might be asked to omit a piece of information in a report, overlook a policy, quietly reduce the established price of a product, or undertake any one of hundreds of other troublesome actions. However, you must first confront the ethical responsibilities in a given situation.

The range of ethical problem-solving strategies available to you is as wide as the range of ethical problems you might encounter over the course of your life. Here are some points to consider as you ponder an ethical dilemma:

1. Understand your responsibility. Sometimes it may be difficult to separate your personal and professional responsibilities. Unless the ethical dilemma involves some civil or criminal liability on your part (or on the part of those around you), an ethical decision in the workplace should be made in light of your professional duties. Still, bear in mind your personal integrity and credibility.

2. Gather facts. Be sure you fully understand the circumstances surrounding the action you're considering. Talk to the people involved, and get as much background information as you need to feel comfortable about your decision.

3. Examine the options. What can you do to resolve the problem and still retain goodwill and the trust of colleagues and clients? The "right" course of action in business today can rarely be stated in simple yes-or-no terms. Your role as an ethical individual is to examine the problem from a variety of angles and to consider a variety of alternative courses.

4. Reframe the problem. Don't look only at the short-term problem and solution. Consider the long-term problem, too. If you take a certain course of action, what benefits or problems may result in the future?

5. Pass the problem along. One of the components of ethical behavior is making other people aware of the problem (and its possible solutions). Don't hesitate to involve other people such as your boss or colleagues. They can shed light on variables you overlook.

6. Play a variety of roles. You might need to be a facilitator, fact gatherer, or arbitrator. Be flexible when troubleshooting with others.

7. Avoid self-righteousness. It rarely solves an ethical problem — and often results in counterproductive emotional arguments and personality disputes.

8. Remember the importance of discussion. Strong ethical behavior implies a willingness to work steadfastly in support of viable solutions. Your willingness to share ideas and to listen to others' views is key to solving the thorniest ethical problems that come your way.

Ethical choices on the job are seldom easy. You must make a choice you can live with. To compromise your own values can damage your self-respect, job satisfaction, and maybe even your career.

ETHICALLY SPEAKING

Should I take some copier paper from work or go buy my own? Should I cover for Jack who wants to take an extra half hour for lunch? Would it be a crime if I just copied last week's results for the maintenance check on this machine if I know it's in top shape?

Choices, choices. We're forced to choose among dozens of them each day. Some decisions, like what we're going to wear to work that day, are governed by everyday considerations, like the weather and what we wore yesterday. But when the choice is between doing what's right and what we know might not be so right, those are ethical dilemmas.

The boss won't be in today. What if I sleep an extra 15 minutes and sneak in a little late? I don't want to talk to this customer. What if I "accidentally" lose the phone message?

Ethics are the moral principles that govern conduct. How we respond in those situations is purely subjective. On the job we may have some guidelines — like rules about safety measures — but even a decision about whether to follow those guidelines is based on our own personal sense of right or wrong — your own code of ethics.

What path do you follow when you're faced with an ethical dilemma? Unfortunately, no simple set of rules can guide every action. Most often, you must rely on the words of Jiminy Cricket, and "let your conscience be your guide." But the Washington, DC-based nonpartisan Character Counts Coalition recently released a list of guidelines they'd like to see more Americans adhere to, both inside and outside the workplace. Follow these suggestions and you'll never have trouble sleeping at night over a decision:

- **Be honest.** Don't mislead or withhold information.

- **Demonstrate integrity.** Resist pressure to do wrong; be your best self. Stand up for what you believe is right or wrong.

- **Keep promises.** Keep your word and honor commitments.

- **Be loyal.** Stand by your family, friends, employers, community, and country. But don't forget to be true to yourself also.

- **Pursue excellence.** Although the quickest road to success is sometimes the devious one, you won't be able to enjoy success for long unless you take the straight and narrow route.

- **Be responsible.** Think before you act; be accountable and "take your medicine."

- **Be kind and caring.** Show you care through generous and compassionate actions.

- **Treat all people with respect.** Be courteous and polite; be tolerant and accepting of individual differences. You can't change people, but you can change your perceptions of them.

- **Be fair.** Treat all people fairly; listen to others and try to understand what they are saying and feeling.

- **Be a good citizen.** Obey the law and respect authority. Follow guidelines to protect the environment.

Still not sure what to do? Wise old Mark Twain may have offered the best advice yet: "Always do right. This will surprise some people and astonish the rest."

PERCEPTION IS EVERYTHING

You think you are credible and display integrity, but your coworkers disagree. Who's right? Your coworkers are right because "we're credible only if others see us that way," says Barbara Pagano, Ed.S., director of Executive Pathways in Roswell, Georgia.

This is important because if people don't think that you or your company are credible, then their opinion of your quality will be low. With so much riding on the perceptions of other people, it makes sense to be aware of how you can build up your own credibility Pagano has the following suggestions:

1. Show courage. We don't usually think of courageousness in connection with our jobs. But look at the people you consider highly credible. How have they shown courage? "We've all done something courageous," Pagano says. Perhaps you've taken a stand for an unpopular idea, for example, or expressed an opinion that no one else dares to voice. A useful team exercise is for each person to think about his or her experiences with courage on the job, and then share them with the group. "I know of a bank examiner who submitted a report and then realized he had made a crucial error," Pagano says. "He showed courage by immediately going to the bank's president and admitting, 'I made a mistake.'"

2. Demonstrate your integrity. We all know it's important not to lie, cheat, or steal. But keeping the "small promises" we make to our teammates, bosses, customers, and other workplace partners is an equally important sign of our integrity. "Too often, we set ourselves up to break our promises," Pagano observes. Because we're eager to please or "come through" for others, we'll say, "I'll get that to you by the end of the day," when we know very well that's impossible. We may forget these small promises we break, but other people don't. Pagano's advice: "Underpromise and overdeliver. You might have to say, for example, 'This week is impossible, but we can have that for you by the middle of next week.' Then be sure you give more than you promised, in this case, by delivering before the deadline you set."

3. Take the initiative to resolve conflicts. "Conflict is natural, and yet so many of us are uncomfortable dealing with it," Pagano observes. "We think we can just ignore it, and it will eventually go away. But proactive individuals are always ready to go to the person or group with whom they're in conflict and say, 'Let's talk about it.' You get a lot of points for doing that."

4. Embrace the chaos of change. "Don't keep yearning for the good old days," Pagano advises. "They're simply not there — and they'll never be again. Of course, we all like security. But things now change so rapidly in organizations, and this accelerated pace of change is expected to continue. Your credibility depends on your ability to see the good in change and to get excited about the possibilities it generates."

SELF-ESTEEM: A MATTER OF DEGREE?

Self-esteem is not a quality that a person either has or doesn't have, says Nathaniel Branden, a Los Angeles-based psychotherapist and management consultant. Instead, Branden claims we all have self-esteem — at least to some degree.

He characterizes low self-esteem as the consequence of a mental and spiritual complacency. A person with low self-esteem tends to avoid frank self-analysis, making hard decisions, or dealing with people in an honest, straightforward (if sometimes painful) way. This is not an effective way to deal with colleagues or customers in the workplace.

If this sounds a little like you, Branden asserts that you can increase your self-esteem — thus your job performance — by practicing several principles:

1. Live consciously. By this Branden means you should be aware of everything going on in your life. If you're only devoting part of your energy and creativity to your job, you should at least acknowledge to yourself that this is the way you're choosing to live. Living life in a fog can become an unhealthy habit.

2. Be self-responsible. Once you've examined your actions and the impact they have, take responsibility as the "author" of your life, says Branden. Your self-esteem will increase as you realize that you control your destiny — not blind luck, fate, or other people. The successes you achieve are your own doing.

3. Be self-accepting. Many people are just too hard on themselves, says Branden. You still can have high self-esteem while accepting that you're just as human as everyone else. This doesn't mean you should shrug off your bad habits or shortcomings. But it does mean that you should have compassion for yourself and respect for your efforts to improve as a person. It also means accepting those parts of yourself, such as certain body characteristics, that you can never change.

4. Be self-assertive. Nobody can read others' minds yet an amazing number of people go through life expecting others to meet their needs. And they're doomed to disappointment. Your self-esteem takes a continuous battering when you don't articulate your needs. Others simply won't understand what you want.

5. Live with a sense of purpose. People with high self-esteem feel that their lives have meaning. And they know that what they do has a strong impact on the lives of others. In the grand scheme, jobs and titles mean nothing — it's how we approach those jobs (and our lives) that makes the difference.

6. Live with integrity. Some people practice deception or a lack of commitment to family, friends, and coworkers (and anyone else for that matter). Deep down, they never gain high self-esteem. They always know in their hearts that what people see is a facade. They wouldn't respect anyone who lied to or cheated on them, so how can they respect themselves?

Sure, all of us feel shaky about ourselves from time to time. It takes practice to admit that we're just as good as anyone else. Your good qualities count to others, so they should matter to you, too. That requires continuous, conscious effort.

Pursue Excellence — Not Perfection

Driven by guilt. That's how many of us feel no matter how much we accomplish. The harder we work, the guiltier we feel. What's going on? "We're trying to do too much, because we want to do it all," says Rebecca Maddox, author of *Inc. Your Dreams* (Viking). "We also want to do it all perfectly, but we can't. That's the origin of these extreme feelings of guilt."

For those of us hounded by guilt, "enough is never enough," she notes. But it should be. "It's time we let up on ourselves." Success is not a matter of how much you do, or being able to do everything perfectly. It's being able to spend your time doing the things that really matter, and pursuing excellence rather than perfection.

To lighten your guilt load:

- **Live by your rules.** Don't base your expectations of yourself on other people's fantasies. We've all heard people talk about how they maintain a high-powered career and a terrific personal partnership, while also being perfect parents and active members of their communities. But, Maddox maintains, "These people are not being truthful. They're living a dangerous fantasy. In the real world, we're sometimes on top of things, and at other times, we can't possibly meet all of our commitments. Trying to live up to another person's fantasies will only make you feel even more inadequate and guilty."

- **Realize that you have more control than you think.** It's not helpful to blame your boss for giving you too much work, Maddox says, or your community for "making" you volunteer so much of your time. It's also futile — and a precursor of burnout — to take the "Gee, if there were only 27 hours in a day, I could do everything I need to do."

  Instead, Maddox advises taking responsibility by acknowledging that you really are the architect of your days. ... We can choose among our many 'priorities.' And we often can say no to the demands of others when they will cause chaos in our personal and/or professional lives.

- **Focus time and energy on what matters most.** Some of us are so determined to do it all that we treat everything as important. Maddox admits she often finds it "very difficult to determine what's really important, and what's not. Everything that crosses my desk seems important." The resulting pressure is "overwhelming and debilitating," she admits.

Pare down to essentials by asking why you're doing a certain task or meeting a particular demand. "You'll be surprised at how many items you can cross off your 'to do' and 'have-to' lists as a result," Maddox says.

"Some things we do simply out of habit, or because everyone else on our street does, or because a former boss once told us to. It's time to stop giving valuable time and energy to tasks that don't require that kind of attention."

STRENGTHEN YOUR CAREER WITH 'SOFT SKILLS'

Whether you're content in your current job or looking for career advancement, you can benefit from developing the "soft skills" perfected by so many highly successful people. Susan B. Wilson, owner of Executive Strategies, an executive training firm in Newton, Iowa, offers these tips:

- **Pursue the authority you need to do your job.** "Effective people are proactive in making sure they have the authority to get things done," Wilson observes. "If you're given extra responsibilities without the commensurate authority, ask for it." Wilson also recommends identifying areas in which you lack the necessary authority. Consider how this is keeping you from meeting company and personal goals, she advises, then seek the authority.

- **Be a skilled problem solver.** "Be the one who identifies problems and offers strategies for resolving them," says Wilson. And be prepared to back up your position with facts and logical arguments. People are more likely to credit you as an expert in your area when you come across as knowing what you're talking about.

- **Prove you are fair and honest.** Show respect for other people's points of view. "You'll be seen as trustworthy if you consistently support a 'win-win' rather than a 'win-lose' result in a conflict or disagreement," Wilson notes. When you make it a priority to put other people in the winner's circle along with you, "you show that you care about their needs as much as your own," she says.

- **Resist the impulse to lash out.** Instead of getting angry with people because you disagree with their opinions or actions, focus on the specific issue that's bothering you. Stop and ask yourself these questions:

What am I really angry about?

To what degree is my pride involved?

What can I do about the situation?

How does my anger benefit my organization?

- **Present ideas at the "right" time.** Even the best ideas will leave people cold if your timing is off, cautions Wilson. "When people are emotionally or intellectually somewhere else, they won't necessarily be responsive to your concerns," she notes. Friday at 4:30 p.m. is not the time to ask a coworker who's eager to get away for the weekend for feedback on your proposal.

- **Use language that reflects reality.** Avoid broad generalizations and absolutes such as "I never arrive late" or "I always listen to others." "People tend to recoil from absolutes because they're rarely true," Wilson explains. "This kind of nit-picking just diverts people from the main topic." Wilson notes that skilled communicators use language that reflects their sense of fairness: "It has been my experience that … " or "In my judgment … ." "In using statements like this, you're acknowledging that others have opinions that may differ from yours," she says.

QUICK TIPS

- **Become a company owner.** Take "ownership" of your company. Define teammates' roles and responsibilities. Members should understand how internal process problems affect customer satisfaction and cost, and be able to identify and compare various opportunities for process improvement within their realms of responsibility.

- **Know your products.** No matter what position you hold with your company, you should know what your products or services do. The best way to gain this knowledge is to use them yourself. Ask your product manager for a hands-on demonstration or trial use so you'll have firsthand knowledge.

- **Professionalism matters most.** Stress professionalism over personality in your relationships with coworkers. While some teammates will be influenced by your sparkling personality, all of them will be impressed by your skill, candor, tact, and professionalism.

- **Be accountable.** No matter how careful you are, mistakes can happen. If they do, maintain your integrity by being accountable. Don't say, "Well, you didn't understand what I said." Instead say, "I'm sorry. I guess I didn't make myself clear."

- **Give the boss a boost.** Let your boss know when you think she has done a good job. Be specific and direct, and you won't seem like a "brownnoser." Bosses need ego boosts too.

- **Sign those phone messages.** Nothing is more frustrating than to need more information about a phone message left on your desk and not to know who it is from. Sign all messages you leave; date them too, in case they become lost in the shuffle.

- **Be a quality advocate.** The next time you witness an example of great service or outstanding quality, call and tell the person responsible how impressed you are. People are so used to getting only "complaint calls" that your positive message will bowl them over and leave them reeling!

- **Check first.** Never make a promise that involves your team at any level without first discussing it with the members. Get everyone together at the same time so that a general consensus can be reached about the promised action. Part of being on a team is thinking and acting as such.

ARE YOU QUALITY-CONSCIOUS?

"We've had a quality-improvement program going in our company for two years, and our senior managers soon are going to give every team an appraisal. Before they do, we as a team want to evaluate our own awareness of what goes into a successful quality program."

— J.J.H., Henderson, Kentucky

Before you sign your name to your team's quality efforts, everyone should be in agreement as to what quality means in general and specifically to your team. This quiz can help you evaluate where you stand today. Have each member read each statement and respond by agreeing or disagreeing. Then check your score and review your answers together.

1. When it comes to quality, there's always room for improvement.   _____

2. Nobody can be aware of quality needs all the time.   _____

3. Customers pay little attention to quality.   _____

4. A quality program must mesh with the organization's goals and profit plans.   _____

5. Quality means conformance to standards.   _____

6. Quality should operate in all parts of a business. _____

7. Personal quality standards and business quality standards have little in common.   _____

8. Quality requires commitment.   _____

9. Quality relates to the process as much as to the goal.   _____

10. People who talk about quality are mostly idealists.   _____

THE PROPER ANSWERS: 1, true; 2, false. Quality doesn't evolve by itself. It requires the constant attention of everyone in the organization; 3, false. Customers today are sophisticated and demanding. They pay as much attention to quality as to price; 4, 5, and 6, true; 7, false. Personal and business quality standards are inseparable. People with high personal standards will be the ones to lead business quality programs. Numbers 8 and 9, true; and 10, false. People who talk about quality are realists. The only way to compete successfully today is to continually improve quality.

The passing grade for this test is 10. If you missed just one answer, your team is failing in at least one key quality area. Concentrate on those statements that you evaluated incorrectly and try to turn your attitude around.

YOUR QUALITY TAKE-AWAY

The Sixth Simple Thing You Can Do for
Your Company and Your Career:

Sign Your Work

Signing your work means you stand behind it. Companies sign their work by offering guarantees and warrantees to their customers. When you're willing to put your personal signature on your work, you're letting the world know that you stand behind your quality. The faith that others have in your quality can lead to promotions and greater career opportunities.

What *You* Can Do

- Always operate in an ethical manner.

- Review your peers' work to guarantee your quality and to show others that you expect quality from them as well.

- Welcome suggestions and criticisms.

- Let others know you value their ideas — the contribution they make can boost their productivity and help increase their personal quality.

- Find ways to work with "difficult" people so that personal feelings don't interfere with the quality you offer customers and suppliers.

- Get the training and education you need to deliver the quality work that's expected of you.

The personal stamp you put on your quality today will carry with you throughout your career.

CHAPTER SEVEN

BENCHMARK THE BEST

"Aim at the sun, and you may not reach it;
but your arrow will fly higher than if you aimed
at an object on a level with yourself."

— J. HOWSE,
AMERICAN BUSINESS WRITER

Introduction

Learning by example. That's the basic element behind one of the biggest quality movements of the day — benchmarking. More specifically, benchmarking is the study of the practices of another organization or organizations, known as partners, in order to improve the quality of processes and increase competitiveness. Companies that have enjoyed success with the technique include benchmarking pioneers like Xerox, Motorola, AT&T, and Alcoa. Because the organizations associated with benchmarking are using well-known giants, it's tempting to think that benchmarking is an activity only they would be interested in.

"That's nonsense," Michael Spiess, executive vice president of the Wallace Company says in *The Bigger Picture,* a publication of the National Society for Quality Control. "Anybody who wants to get better can do it." Wallace Company was a 1990 winner of the Malcolm Baldrige Award — only the second small business to be so honored. Wallace is a distributor of pipes, valves, fittings, and specialty products primarily for the chemical and petrochemical industries, with 280 employees and annuals sales of approximately $90 million.

Benchmarking, Spiess says, has proved its value as a way to maintain the competitive edge. "It's a real eye opener," he says. "One of the things you must do if you're going to be a successful is have a very open mind about everything you do. When you open up your mind and really start to look at something, you find you consistently want to improve. And the fastest way we know how to do that is by benchmarking."

Benchmarking can also take place between departments and between teams. But you can also use benchmarking to "learn from the best" on a personal level. One such way is by taking on a mentor in your department or company. A mentor is a knowledgeable, often influential individual who takes an interest in and advises another person concerning that person's career.

Mentors are integral to successful career advancement. A study at General Motors found that all the upper-level managers had at least one mentor in their careers and they credited their mentors for guiding their career advancement. Through your mentor, you can compare your decisions and choices against the best.

To learn more about benchmarking, read on.

WHAT WOULD YOU DO?

SMALL FIRMS CAN BE BIG BENCHMARKERS

You own a small manufacturing company with a growing product line. You'd like to become even better through benchmarking. However, some of your team members think that only big, industrial organizations can perform the process properly.

Small and growing, big and booming — the size of a company doesn't matter when it comes to benchmarking. Robert Camp contends that small organizations can use the same techniques that he implemented at Xerox in the 1980s.

Camp is now the company's manager of benchmark competence. He's also the author of two books: *Benchmarking* and *Business Process Benchmarking* (both ASQC Quality Press). "The objectives are the same for both large and small companies," Camp says in *Industry Week*. "They're constantly striving to improve, and one way to do that is to learn from others. The essence of benchmarking is simply finding and implementing the best practices to get improved results."

Because so many large corporations have drastically reduced their supplier rosters, small firms that buy from numerous sources actually have a much wider range of potential partners. And, if the vendors are local, the company can conduct your studies without the travel expenses that big benchmarkers often incur. Also, if some members of the organization belong to a service club, like Kiwanis or Rotary, the contacts they make in their clubs may turn up leads on local benchmarking "targets." The key is to find an operation whose processes are compatible with the firm's.

"You must identify partners from a process point of view," Camp stresses. "For example, when Xerox benchmarked L.L. Bean's order-fulfillment process, many people saw it as a mismatch in terms of overall size. In fact, for that process, Bean was an even match for us. Large companies often have many individual operations in different locations that are equal matches for smaller companies."

Camp cites three benchmarking basics to get a small firm started:

1. Decide what should be benchmarked. You can't ask a partner firm to outline its entire technological process. Select one phase, learn it, and then cover another procedure.

2. Look for companies outside your own industry. They'll be more cooperative and may have processes that can be integrated into your business.

3. Be prepared. Gather as much information as you can from public sources before you visit your partner.

"Benchmarking is a quality tool," Camp observes. "It's one more way to help you improve. Large or small, if you don't learn from others, how are you going to grow?"

A GOOD START ENCOURAGES BENCHMARK SUCCESS

The success of a benchmarking team's efforts will depend largely on how well members handle the early planning stages, says Diane Andrews, leadership and quality development specialist with Texas Instruments in Dallas. Andrews offers these suggestions when you benchmark:

- **Document everything you do.** "That way, you'll never have to go back and try to remember exactly what you did," Andrews explains. Your documentation should begin with details of the process you've selected to study; why you chose that process; the scope and objectives of the project; critical measurements used in your process; and potential payoffs of the study.

- **Research potential benchmarking partners.** "This is an extensive process that initially involves compiling a list of potential partners — perhaps as many as 20," says Andrews. Then, through investigating your own process and those of potential partners, you'll be narrowing your list down to three or four who have the best practices in the process you're benchmarking.

Once you have developed a core list, Andrews offers these tips:

- **Use the library.** Annual reports, position papers, business directories, and industry and business periodicals can all educate you about potential partners. If you find a particularly interesting article, call the author to see if you can find more information or get a contact name within the featured company.

- **Cross-check data.** Don't select a potential partner on the basis of one piece of information. If you read about a company that's doing very well with the process you want to benchmark, go one step further. Call someone in the company to verify that its process is similar enough to your own to make a benchmarking partnership fruitful.

- **Design a questionnaire for potential partners.** Their responses will help you narrow your initial "potentials" list considerably. "Base your questions closely on your own process," suggests Andrews, "specifically what you want to find out that the others do differently." The questionnaire should help identify potential partners whose processes have enough similarities to yours that their best practices could be incorporated into your own process.

- **Call ahead to make initial contacts.** Advises Andrews: "Let them know what you're doing: 'We're launching a benchmarking study of our warehousing cycle-time process. We'd like to send you a questionnaire to see if we might share some information with you based on our process.'"

- **Plan well for site visits.** "You don't want to waste either their time or your own," Andrews says. Your visiting team should include a spokesperson to act as the team voice; a recorder to document everything said or done during the visit; and an observer to act as an extra set of eyes and ears.

- **Set up an appointment** for a visit well in advance.

- **Prepare questions and forward them** before your visit to give the other team a chance to prepare responses.

- **Forward all relevant details** regarding how you handle your own process. Provide any information about your process that you are expecting other companies to give you about theirs.

- **After examining all collected data, select your partner or partners.** Ask yourself: "What is it about their process that makes it a best practice?" Andrews cautions that a best practice may work only for a particular process in a specific company. Choose benchmarking partners whose best practices will be most applicable to your own process.

Benchmark Ethics

Your team is taking part in a benchmarking program to compare your organization's quality guidelines to those of other organizations in your industry. But what kind of information is acceptable to ask for — and how to go about asking for it?

These are among the ethical questions every organization should ask itself before launching a benchmarking effort, says Michael Spendolini, Ph.D., founder of MJS Associates, an organizational development consulting and training firm, and author of *The Benchmarking Book* (AMACOM). Spendolini's golden rule of benchmarking activities: "Never request information you would not give." He provides additional guidelines to follow:

- **Put all agreements in writing.** Draw up a general benchmarking agreement and then tailor it to each individual partner, if necessary. Include a nondisclosure clause stating what information is not accessible to benchmarkers.

- **Treat all benchmarking data as confidential.** Never discuss information gathered from one benchmarking partner with another, unless you have permission in writing. You'll lose one partner's trust and could run into legal problems.

- **Disclose your intentions.** Unless the information you are gathering is available to the general public — in annual reports, for example — benchmarkers must identify their organizations and the purpose of their requests for data. This also applies to plant tours not normally given to the general public.

- **Be careful when exchanging price or market-share information.** You probably don't need to worry about this aspect when you're looking for quality-related data. However, it's still important to know that benchmarking price or market-share data with competitors may result in a violation of the Sherman Antitrust Act, which attempts to prevent price-fixing among the market's major competitors, says Spendolini.

- **Respect personal relationships.** Don't take advantage of relationships you may have developed with individuals at organizations you are benchmarking. "Never ask them to reveal information as a personal favor," notes Spendolini, or under the pretext that it will be "just between you and me." You must show respect for their principles.

Every organization involved in benchmarking should have a code of ethics, says Spendolini, to govern the practices of employees gathering data. Such a code shows your benchmarking partners that you're serious about establishing a professional and fair relationship with them.

BENCHMARK OTHER DEPARTMENTS

To gain a good understanding of your team's or your department's quality objectives, you may not have to look outside your own group. You'll get a much clearer view by visiting other departments, says Philip B. Crosby the father of the "zero-defects" quality movement. "I've observed that most first-line people aren't aware of what others are doing," remarks Crosby. "I recently visited factories in India, Greece, and Korea, and was surprised to see how much input hourly workers have in the quality process there. "The better manufacturers there are picking up on what the top American organizations are doing to bring workers into the quality-control picture. Most employers in North America still need to learn the same lessons from the quality leaders," he notes.

If your team is isolated from other operations, schedule tours of departments that are involved in different types of work, suggests Crosby. Begin by visiting the sector that is most closely allied to yours. Then, move on to other parts of your workplace. Eventually you'll understand how each operation is linked to the next one. "This is particularly important if there have been recent changes in your systems or product line," Crosby notes. "If a reorganization is under way, it's critical that you keep up-to-date. How much time you spend visiting other departments largely depends on the size of your company. In most plants, such a 'round-robin' tour could be conducted in a day or two," he says.

Ideal tour groups would be comprised of members of unrelated teams. "Show-and-tell" instruction should be conducted by a quality engineer. For example, say you're a member of a machinist team. Have you ever wondered what happens to the results of your work after it leaves your production area? A "go-with-the-flow" tour would give you new insights into the whole process.

Finally, seek guided tours of such departments as purchasing, personnel, finance, shipping, engineering, and design. Soon, everything will emerge as a mosaic of interconnected pieces. What you'll end up with is an understanding of the "big picture" of your company's quality operations.

Need New Ideas?
Look *Outside* Your Industry

As creative as your team may be, outside thinking is invaluable. Looking beyond your own company and industry for processes that can be adapted to your uses is the basis for successful benchmarking.

"Insiders think about improving what already exists, but outsiders bring fresh possibilities," explains Paul Friedman, editor of *The Pryor Report*. He offers these examples:

1. While Swiss watchmakers continually improved the quality of their mechanical timepieces, outsiders discovered that watches would run better through the use of microprocessors.

2. The electronic calculator was developed outside the slide-rule industry.

3. Copper telephone wires now are being replaced by optical fibers, microwave dishes, and satellites. None of these were

created by research-and-development staffs within the tele-phone industry.

At the Massachusetts Institute of Technology in Cambridge, professor Steven Kim studied 58 major inventions that came from Europe and America. They included photography, com-puters, and ball-point pens. "Among these innovations," Friedman says, "at least 46 originated from individuals or orga-nizations other than the key companies in the mainstream industries."

10 QUESTIONS

Suppose you're preparing to benchmark another company to learn its best processes. What procedure might you follow?

Here is a list of 10 questions a team from Xerox asked its employees in its benchmarking program. You might want to use these as a starting point as you model your own questions:

1. What factor is most critical to our company's success?

2. What factors are causing the most trouble?

3. What products or services are provided?

4. What factors account for customer satisfaction?

5. What specific operational problems have been identi-fied in the organization?

6. Where are our competitive pressures felt most strongly?

7. What operations account for our biggest expenses?

8. Which operations represent the highest percentage of our costs?

9. Which functions most need to be improved?

10. Which products or services have the greatest potential to separate us from our competitors?

As you seek answers, remember the most vital areas: cost and problem reduction; customer satisfaction; continuous improvement; and market superiority.

CAREER BOOSTER: BENCHMARK YOUR OWN COMPANY

One of the ways personal benchmarking can benefit you most is by utilizing it right there in your own company. Every company is different, not only in the products or services it provides, but in subtle ways as well. At one company, a quiet professional manner is rewarded; at another, those who succeed most are those with a "go grab the world" attitude.

Understanding the subtle differences and adjusting your behavior to fit can be a key to getting ahead at your company and to move forward in your career. Using your best benchmarking skills, you can gain an objective view of your organization and put what you've learned to work for you.

"Knowing what makes your organization tick is important in your career marketing goals," says Jeffrey P. Davidson, in *Blow Your Own Horn (How to Get Noticed — and Get Ahead)* (Berkley)."Realistically assessing your company's policies and procedures and the underlying rationale for them will enable you to know how to get ahead in the atmosphere that prevails."

Here are some ways to benchmark your organization's practices:

- **Watch walls and bulletin boards.** Many companies hang awards on the walls. Normally, you might walk right past them. But during your benchmarking investigation, slow down and look more closely. If your company has been awarded plaques or awards from outside organizations, you can learn which companies, community groups, or organizations are important to the image of the company. On the other hand, "If the awards are from your company to its own employees, they will tell you the characteristics and skills valued by the company," says Davidson.

Bulletin boards, too, reveal a lot about your company. Suggestion boxes indicate that your company values input from its workers. "A bulletin board with notices from management — but no opportunity for employee input — tells a different story," says Davidson

- **Check out the reception areas.** Look for magazines on the coffee tables. If there is a mix of travel magazines, it's a good indication your company takes a global approach to business.

- **Read the policy manual.** In addition to the mundane procedural matters it covers, the manual may include discussion of company goals, responsibilities of different positions, and promotion polices — all valuable information for helping you get ahead.

- **Survey the lunch room.** "Use lunches as an opportunity to meet and get to know other people in your organization, especially those in divisions that complement yours or to which you might someday be interested in transferring," suggests the author.

- **Notice organizational communication patterns.** Is there an open atmosphere where everyone is encouraged to make a contribution? Davidson once benchmarked a General Motors plant in Brookhaven, Mississippi. He was impressed with the degree of dialogue he witnessed. "Besides the usual communications such as a monthly newspaper, frequent meetings of employees teams, and an electronic news display in the cafeteria, management at the facility holds quarterly meetings for all employees," says Davidson. "Such open dialogue keeps productivity high and turnover low."

- **Take part in training programs.** "Each and every time you attend a training session, you are increasing your overall market value," says Davidson. "What you learn in those sessions may well support your existing or future goals."

As you can see, a little benchmarking of your own company can uncover some interesting and useful information.

PERSONAL BENCHMARKING WITH A MENTOR

Mentors can be a key to success in your current job and in your career. Whether or not your career aspirations include executive management, having a mentor can help you succeed. This is because mentors:

- **Guide.** They map out the politics and political climate of the company for you.

- **Advise.** They support you during difficult times.

- **Counsel.** They act as a sounding board and recommend action items to solve problems.

- **Coach.** They encourage, advise, and build confidence.

- **Serve as role models.** They set an example of how to behave in various situations.

Linking up with a mentor is an excellent way to benchmark on a personal level. Your personal quality will be strengthened as you compare your own best practices with those of a seasoned pro.

Here is a quick question and answer guide to finding a mentor:

1. Can a boss be a mentor? Your boss is often not the best choice for a mentor. A mentor and protégé have a special relationship. A boss-subordinate mentoring relationship may be perceived as "playing favorites." A better choice: Someone in another part of the organization who is familiar with your work.

2. Can I have more than one mentor? Many individuals in the General Motors study noted they had multiple mentors. Different people may help you in different ways.

3. How often will I see my mentor? You might meet only when you need to. But some people talk to their mentors every other month, and others more often.

4. Do I need to take the mentor's advice? You don't have to follow advice, but you should tell your mentor what you decide to do and why. Also, listen when your mentor sounds very concerned or even alarmed about a situation. His or her experience will probably send up a red flag to a problem before you know it.

5. Can the opposite sex be a good mentor? Absolutely. But both the mentor and the protégé must remember to have meetings in a very straightforward manner and tell spouses, secretaries, and fellow workers what is going on to ward off rumors. Females are hard-pressed to find female mentors, thus having a male mentor is more likely.

6. Will I outgrow my mentor? Protégés often outgrow their mentors. A good mentor recognizes this and celebrates the graduation to independence. Some mentors have enough self confidence to recommend a next-step mentor.

A final piece of advice: Don't be afraid to ask someone you admire to be your mentor. If the person agrees, you will grow personally as well as professionally.

KNOW THE LANGUAGE

As with most quality team initiatives, benchmarking has developed a vocabulary all its own. And the first rule of getting along in a foreign land is learning how to speak the language.

How well do you speak benchmarking? Match up the following numbered benchmarking phrases with their lettered definitions, as defined by author Gregory H. Watson in *Strategic Benchmarking* (John Wiley and Sons, Inc.):

1. Best-in-class

    a. Outstanding process performance within an activity regardless of industry

2. Best practice

    b. Radical redesign of business processes

3. Core competency

    c. Critical practices that influence customers' perception of your business

4. Key business process

    d. Outstanding process performance within an industry

5. Re-engineering

    e. Strategic business capabilities that provide an organization with a marketplace advantage

ANSWERS:

1: d; 2: a; 3: e; 4: c; 5: b. One of the best ways to improve your benchmarking vocabulary is to read up on the subject. The business section of your local bookstore is sure to have several books to choose from. Make a commitment yourself to keep learning.

CUSTOMERS DRIVE ISO 9000 REGISTRATION

Customers and quality — not the European market — seem to be the driving forces behind many companies' efforts to receive ISO 9000 registration. This finding is just one from a recent survey of companies in the United States and Canada that are registered with ISO 9000. The 35-question survey, conducted by Quality Systems Update (QSU) and Deloitte & Touche, a consulting firm, asked some of the most common questions posed by companies considering registration.

"This survey of ISO 9000-registered companies, the first of its type, provides valuable insights into the registration process and what the registered companies have experienced," says Howard Danford, president of CEEM, Inc., which publishes *Quality Systems Update*. Here are some of the findings, as reported in QSU:

Survey results seem to refute the widely held assertion that the dramatic rise in the popularity of ISO 9000 is due to companies' desire to be in line with European requirements. Only 9 percent of respondents cited the European community requirements as the primary reason for their pursuit of registration.

Instead, customer demands and expectations were listed most often, followed closely by quality benefits. Other top reasons, in order: market advantage; corporate mandate; part of larger company strategy often related to pursuit of a Malcolm Baldrige award; competitive pressures; and reduced costs of production.

ISO 9000 registration quickly earned a reputation for being a paper- and procedure-laden process. In keeping with that image, respondents listed procedure creation and document development as the two greatest obstacles to registration.

Other problems cited were lack of management commitment; not following set procedures; employee resistance; and conflicting interpretations. Despite these barriers, more companies apply for ISO 9000 every year because of the many benefits.

External benefits considered most significant were higher perceived quality from customers and vendors; a higher level of customer satisfaction; and a better, stronger competitive edge. The top three internal benefits listed were better recordkeeping or documentation; a greater awareness of quality by all employees; and a positive "cultural change" within the company.

ISO 9000 EVEN BENEFITS SMALL COMPANIES

Can ISO 9000 certification — the quality benchmark established by the Switzerland-based International Organization for Standardization — help a smaller company? Paula Rice, president of Veritas, a quality consulting and training firm in Hauppage, New York, thinks so and tells the story of Rice Aircraft, an aviation-industry hardware supplier that she owns. It operates out of Hauppage and Medley, Florida.

"Companies have been slow to embrace the idea of quality standards because they think ISO accreditation takes too long and costs too much," Rice says. "Today, small and midsize companies can achieve certification within 12 to 18 months, with moderate expenditures. And, any company looking to compete in the global marketplace has to be ISO-accredited. You'll run the extreme risk of being shut out of the market without the ISO 9000 seal of approval."

Rice brought Rice Aircraft through the certification procedure within 10 months of the time that she filed in. Through intensive cross training, she says, the company has cut its waste by 30 percent. With only 29 people on the payroll, Rice Aircraft won the 1993 Blue Chip Enterprise Initiative Award from the U.S. Chamber of Commerce. It's the first aviation-industry firm of its kind to earn ISO 9000 certification.

UNDERSTANDING QUALITY:
ISO 9000 VS. TQM

Quality — that's the bottom line. Management may call your plant's current quality effort total quality management (TQM) or ISO 9000, but should the name of the program make a difference to you, as long as you achieve bottom-line results? The answer is yes.

If you think of TQM and ISO 9000 as programs, you are bound to be confused and frustrated. They aren't programs. And they don't conflict with each other. Understanding the differences will help you and your team better understand your roles in achieving quality and in meeting your quality goals.

The connection between TQM and ISO 9000 becomes clearer when you consider the evolution of the following four stages of quality thinking, as described by David Garvin of the Harvard Business School:

1. Inspection. Quality management focuses on the product. Inspectors who sort out defects are responsible for quality.

2. Quality control. The focus remains on the product and production process, but statistical techniques to reduce variability are introduced. Manufacturing and engineering become responsible for quality.

3. Quality assurance. At this stage, the entire production chain (from design to delivery) becomes responsible for quality. Prevention, rather than detection, is the prevalent notion.

4. Strategic quality or TQM. The focus shifts from the product and production process to the market and customers. Senior management assumes responsibility for quality.

Each stage represents a philosophy that drives your company's quality system. And every organization has a quality system, which is the philosophy and procedures by which an organization conducts itself to satisfy customers and to comply with all other operational requirements.

How does ISO 9000 fit in? ISO 9000 is a series of international standards for assessing quality management systems used by manufacturing companies. It does not focus on quality results achieved.

TQM and ISO 9000 address similar aspects of quality management, but emphasize different things. TQM focuses more on human resources issues. ISO 9000 emphasizes quality process issues. ISO 9000 ensures that the road to achieving quality is paved with proven systems.

A comprehensive quality process that is recognized and accepted by manufacturers around the world requires both TQM and ISO 9000. An organization can be ISO-registered and effectively produce and deliver the wrong products or services. TQM is essential to assure that the "right" products and services are effectively delivered to the customer.

10 QUALITY BENCHMARKS

"Strong total-quality programs are like strong stomachs," A.V. Feigenbaum says. "They work best when you scarcely know they're there." Feigenbaum, president and CEO of General Systems Company Inc., in Pittsfield, Massachusetts, has been a prominent advocate of "total quality control" for more than 40 years.

There are, he says, 10 basic benchmarks for total quality success. If your program is going to work, quality must be:

1. A company-wide process. Technical capability isn't the principal quality problem facing companies today, Feigenbaum observes: "What differentiates the quality leaders from the followers is quality discipline and clear quality-work processes. Everyone in the organization must understand, believe in, and be a part of them."

2. Geared to customer needs. Quality, the General Systems CEO says, isn't what an engineer, marketer, or general manager wants. "If you want to find out about quality," he contends, "go out and ask your customer. Nobody can compress in a market-research statistic the buyer frustration caused by a water leak in a new car."

3. A cost-saver. Quality products and services generate sizable savings through waste reduction. "Quality cost," Feigenbaum says, "has become today's best return-on-investment corporate performer."

4. The result of both personal and team effort. "Quality is everybody's job, but will be nobody's unless all the left hands work with all the right hands," the quality pioneer maintains. "The biggest problem in many programs is that they are quality improvement islands without bridges."

5. A way of managing. Good quality management means making everyone realize that, when quality is right, everything else will be right, too.

6. A product-development partner. "From the start, quality must be a partner of product development," Feigenbaum notes. "It's not a sweep-up-after mechanism for development problems."

7. A corporate ethic. A deep recognition that what you're doing is right, he stresses, is the strongest human motivation. It's the driving force behind quality leadership.

8. Improving steadily. "There's no such thing as a permanent quality level," according to Feigenbaum. "Quality is a constantly upward-moving target. I think of continuous improvement as the jogging-and-fitness discipline for quality leadership."

9. The most economical route to productivity. Bad work is the greatest and most costly obstacle to profitable output. You and your teammates must think in terms of good rather than more.

10. Part of a total system. Your customers and suppliers must be involved. "This is what makes quality leadership real," Feigenbaum emphasizes. "Systematic methodology makes it possible for you to manage quality — not just let it happen."

FIND A QUALITY 'RECIPE'
THAT WORKS FOR YOU

"Recipe" is a good word to use to describe the process of creating a quality program. If they don't have the right ingredients right from the very start, even the best chefs in the world won't be able to create anything palatable. In *Quality Progress* magazine, Roland A. Dumas uses the baking analogy to describe how most companies approach implementing quality programs: "Find an expert and ask what ingredient is key to a good cake. Get that ingredient and bake it. Throw it out. Find another expert and ask what ingredient he believes is most critical. Get that ingredient and bake it. Throw out the mess. Repeat."

This parallels companies' experiences with quality programs in that "when the program does not achieve the desired outcome, it is replaced by that of another guru, and so forth," says Dumas. To avoid this cycle, include Dumas' ingredients, as reported by Patrick E. Townsend and Joan E. Gebhardt, authors of *Quality in Action* (John Wiley & Sons), in your quality recipe:

1. Training, first and foremost. Before new systems and technologies can be introduced, the people who will be using them — the frontiers — require training. Otherwise, you have a great new quality system in place and no one capable of operating it.

2. Change driving change. Technical change should drive social change and vice-versa. Unless there are alterations in the corporate culture, progress will be stalled, and people will become frustrated with the program.

3. Basic beginnings. "The definition of quality should related to everyone's job," says Dumas. "It should be simple and practical." If no one can explain quality in their own words, they missed the basics.

4. Internal experts. Don't let the quality theorists make all your decisions. Learn from them, but be guided by your own organizational needs.

5. Broader vision. Look beyond your workplace and industry. Broaden your scope by studying how others handle such matters as quality training, hiring, promotion, and customer satisfaction.

6. "Value-drive" approach. Don't get so caught up in specifications, modifications, and measurements that you forget what quality is all about. "Above all, quality is an ethic — a value more important than financial return," Dumas says.

A partial understanding of quality produces either partial success or total failure. To get a complete picture, reshuffle the ingredients of your recipe to find the mix that works best for you.

<u>IDEA IN ACTION</u>

LIFE AFTER BALDRIGE

For companies that have won the Malcolm Baldrige National Quality Award, the honor isn't an empty showpiece to hang on the boardroom wall. It's an investment in quality that has excellent returns. The National Institute of Standards and Technology, which administers the award, offers these examples of quality returns experienced by past award winners as a result of implementing quality programs and procedures:

- Granite Rock has seen customer accounts increase 38 percent from 1989 through 1993, while overall construction spending declined 40 percent.

- Texas Instruments Defense Systems & Electronics Group experienced a 21 percent reduction in production cycle time in 1992, with a 56 percent reduction in stock-to-production time.

- Federal Express has achieved significant savings since 1986: $27 million in personnel; $1.5 million in recovered revenue by a computer automation team; and $462,000 in saved overtime payments.

- Motorola has seen employee productivity improve 100 percent over the past six years.

- AT&T Transmission Systems Business Unit reduced time to market by 50 percent in three years.

In all these success stories, of course, the quality programs instituted in preparation for Malcolm Baldrige judging — not the award itself — turned out to be the real prize.

IDEA IN ACTION

QUALITY TEAM CONTENDERS SHARE GOLDEN TRAITS

One way to evaluate your work team is to compare it against teams that have won The National Team Excellence Awards Competition. The competition is held every spring by the Association for Quality and Participation (AQP) and honors work teams the same way the Malcolm Baldrige National Quality Award recognizes companies.

In 1985, AQP presented its first National Team Excellence Award. When Texaco Refining and Marketing, Inc., took home the 1995 prize, it received an honor that has become as coveted by teams as the Malcolm Baldrige Award is by companies. During that decade of winners, all AQP gold medal holders shared certain characteristics, notes Jo Ann Jones, manager of member and chapter services for AQP and the association's award administrator. Whether your team wants to receive public quality recognition or a private victory of excellence, you can learn from their example.

"Each of our winners has excelled at beginning with a strong problem-solving process and following through until final team decisions are made," Jones explains. "They succeed by getting input from their customers, suppliers, and other stockholders. Members of our winning teams also are highly skilled communicators," she notes.

Three types of teams have taken the AQP laurels. *Problem solvers* strive to determine the roots of difficulties and cause-and-effect relationships. *Improvement teams* work to create a better organizational product, service, or system. *Innovative teams* develop or install new concepts.

"There's no ideal team size. Our winners have had as few as three members and as many as 18," notes Jones. "The strongest entrants are those that have received training from many different people. Team leaders typically play coordinating or facilitative roles."

Just as the AQP winners share common traits, so do the losers. Teams that are almost certain to fail, Jones says, consist of people who are taking on team functions as an extra job duty instead of The National Teams Award, an ongoing one. "Success comes only when the teamwork process is part of the company culture," she notes. "If senior managers want their teams to be serious contenders, they must have a real commitment to and belief in teamwork. Winners represent companies in which management passes enthusiasm on to team members."

Whether you want to prove your team's quality greatness to the whole country or to yourselves, following the traits of recognized winners can point you in the right direction.

JUDGE FOR YOURSELF

How does your team measure against the best? Benchmark your team against these three teams. They are recent winners of the Association for Quality and Participation (AQP) National Team Excellence Awards.

Gold medal: "Impact 7," an employee team from Texaco Refining and Marketing, Inc., in Bellaire, Texas. The company refines and markets motor gasoline, diesel fuel, and lubricating oil. It's also responsible for credit-card processing and marketing activities in the United States.

Impact 7 set out to streamline the process Texaco uses to send 600 various letters to its credit card customers. Its goal: to increase productivity, reduce departmental expenses, and improve customer satisfaction. As a result of its efforts, Impact 7 reduced the number of customer complaints by 40 percent. Annually, the company saved 7,000 employee work hours and $100,000.

Silver medal: "Starch-A-Techs," a team from Grain Processing Corporation in Muscatine, Iowa. The team took on the challenge of improving the company's inlet air-filter systems. Its efforts slashed filter costs by $406,000, improved safety, and boosted operator morale.

Bronze medal: "Automation Enhancers" from Diamond Star Motors in Normal, Illinois. The team tackled a problem caused by mold-change operations. By fully automating the mixhead handling and change process, all accidents related to the operation were eliminated. Diamond Star's team also brought about significant reductions in annual operating, material, and equipment costs. In addition, the time required to change each mold was cut by 18 minutes.

Quick Tips

- **Do it the best way you know how.** Efficiency is doing your work the best way you know how, rather than in a way that's better for someone else. Although benchmarking your peers can give you good ideas, don't stick with them if they don't work for you. A good work process is a personal issue.

- **Look ahead.** How valuable are weekly or monthly reports that tell only what your team has accomplished? Make the reports more helpful to the leadership by adding what the team expects to accomplish within the next 30 to 60 days. The next report can cite results based on those goals.

- **Benchmark locally.** Another good place to begin your benchmarking efforts is with another team within your organization. If there is another group doing what your team does, only better, benchmark to learn from their successes as well as from your team's failures.

- **Avoid pessimists.** Pessimists often target newcomers to gripe to about the organization. Why? Because often new coworkers are too polite to ignore them. This can kill morale and lead to higher turnover. Head off pessimists by presenting a positive impression to new peers. Although you can't stop pessimists from spreading the gloom, you can offer a brighter perspective.

- **Avoid excuses.** When another group is benchmarking your team, avoid using the word "because" when explaining something it did. Listeners assume that excuses and assumptions will follow. *Better:* "We did this, which resulted in ... "

- **Try the Swiss cheese approach.** When your team can't reach a consensus in solving a problem, "Approach the problem as you would a slice of Swiss cheese, taking several bites at a time," suggests Thomas Kayers in his book *Building Team Power* (Irwin). "Break the problem into issues and solve it one issue at a time. By taking several bites, and putting a few holes in the slice, the problem will not seem so oppressive."

- **Prepare to bench.** If you're involved in a benchmarking relationship with another organization, find out everything you can about them before your first meeting. In addition, fax your contact information about your company. You'll save previous meeting time by having already covered the basics in advance.

HOW MUCH DO YOU KNOW ABOUT BENCHMARKING?

"We're about to contact another company about being our partner in a benchmarking effort. This is new to us. We don't want our partners to think we're complete novices at this! Help us make sure we understand the concept."

— P.W., Austin, Texas

A benchmark is a point of reference from which measurements can be made. It is also a standard of comparison used in business to improve efficiency and effectiveness. When companies benchmark, they identify success stories, both inside and outside their own industries, and adapt what they learn to their own businesses. To test your knowledge of benchmarking basics, respond (a), (b), or (c) to the following statements:

1. A primary reason companies benchmark is to:
    (a) cut marketing costs;
    (b) improve the quality and performance of critical operations;
    (c) get a larger share of the market.   ____

2. When benchmarking, a company must be wary of:
    (a) getting carried away with "being the best";
    (b) turning off potential customers with overpriced products;
    (c) reaching invalid conclusions from a benchmarking study. ____

3. Which of the following is a good reason for benchmarking?
    (a) to learn if an operation is on par with "the best";
    (b) to determine if you can cut costs;
    (c) to find ways to increase productivity.   ____

4. A critical step in using benchmarking as a quality strategy is to:
    (a) compare your company's performance only with that of companies in your industry;
    (b) limit implementing new practices to those that bring about immediate benefits;
    (c) measure differences in performance precisely so you can place most of your efforts in the areas where they are most needed.   ____

5. Companies that successfully benchmark benefit because:
   (a) the study is headed by a manager who is skilled in the
       strategy and technique;
   (b) the benchmarking procedure uses a logical method
       for developing winning policies and plans;
   (c) management hires a consultant to conduct the study.   ____

THE CORRECT ANSWERS ARE: 1: (b); 2: (a) and (c); 3: (a); 4: (c); 5: (b). Before you launch a benchmarking endeavor, be sure you and everyone on your team fully understands the process and what's involved.

YOUR QUALITY TAKE-AWAY

The Seventh Simple Thing You Can Do for
Your Company and Your Career:

Benchmark the Best

Role models come in all shapes and sizes. And they can be found anywhere in the world by anyone willing to conduct a systematic search. One way to do it is by benchmarking — a process for measuring an organization, a department, or an individual's current status by comparing it either to past performance or to the accomplishments of others. Small companies as well as large organizations can benefit from benchmarking. An organization can look from within its own industry or to an outside industry for a benchmarking partner. The key is to find comparable areas to benchmark. Another way organizations measure quality is through awards or certifications such as ISO 9000 registration.

What *You* Can Do

Benchmarking can help you do your current job better and point you in the right direction as you make long-term decisions about your career.

- Find a mentoring partner at work. A mentor can serve as a role model and guide as you chart your career path.

- Benchmark others in your organization on an informal basis. Watch the leaders in your organization and learn what skills and traits helped them move ahead in the organization.

- Learn from the best in your profession. Read profiles in business publications. Study the successes of winners." Glean all you can from their experiences.

- Benchmark your own company. Observe your organization the way you would analyze an outside company you were benchmarking. Learn about such matters as your company's values and the importance it places on communication. What does it take to succeed in your organization? Adjusting your behavior to fit your organization's needs is the key to getting ahead at your company.

PART II

TIPS AND TECHNIQUES FOR

• SUPERVISORS

• CUSTOMER SERVICE REPS

• SECRETARIES AND OFFICE SUPPORT STAFF

CHAPTER EIGHT

SUPERVISING FOR A QUALITY PERFORMANCE

"If anything goes bad, I did it.
If anything goes semi-good, then we did it.
If anything goes real good, then you did it.
That's about all it takes to get people to win football games."
— PAUL "BEAR" BRYANT (1913–1983),
AMERICAN COLLEGE FOOTBALL COACH

INTRODUCTION

Your most important responsibility as a supervisor is to bring out a quality performance from your staff. To bring out the best in others, you need to have the respect of those who you supervise. Think for a moment, about a former supervisor whom you considered especially effective. That individual probably stands out in your mind because he or she was likable and approachable.

Although supervising isn't a popularity contest and the skills and traits that make an individual "likable" and "approachable" are not always included in traditional supervisory development programs, by boosting them you can increase your own effectiveness. Here are guidelines to help you achieve success as a supervisor:

- **Develop a sense of identity.** Knowing who you are and what you want to do is invaluable in pursuing a satisfying career and living a good life.

- **Acquire cross-cultural sensitivity.** The United States remains a melting pot of cultural, racial, and ethnic diversity. These multiple origins have impacted attitudes, motivations, and dreams. Learn to celebrate the differences in your employees as a wealth of opportunity and recognize how those differences can contribute to the workplace.

- **Develop cultural and moral humility.** Personally effective individuals accept that not everyone shares the same point of view. And they accept these differences of opinion, even if they do not agree with them.

- **Don't "finger-point" when problems occur.** Instead of spending time trying to assign blame for a problem, work to resolve problems at their core.

- **Become flexible.** Quality improvement in the workplace requires flexibility. The best supervisors and managers are those who understand their organization's quality goals and processes and translate them into action steps for their employees. Good bosses accept failure and reward people for trying.

- **Learn how to negotiate.** Negotiation skills include being able to read body language, listen actively, test assumptions, and organize thoughts. These skills are applicable to all phases of work and your personal life.

- **Develop diplomacy.** Tact requires focusing on making others comfortable and taking care not to embarrass a person in front of someone else. Few people reach leadership positions without refining their diplomatic skills.

- **Develop repair strategies and skills.** If you make a mistake in a relationship, have a plan for restoring the relationship to its original level. For example, statements such as "I did not intend to make you look foolish," or "I am responsible for the mistake, not you, and I am sorry you were blamed" go a long way toward restoring trust. Long-term relationships require trust, and trust requires effort, time, honesty, and continuous dialogue. The ability to fix a relationship reaps lifelong rewards.

- **Practice patience.** Rushing is a great enemy in today's business world. If you hurry to finish a task, you often miss important details that will make a critical difference. The best (and perhaps only) way to develop patience is to practice it: Put yourself in difficult and trying circumstances such as driving in rush hour traffic, waiting in a bank line, and carefully listening to a disgruntled employee and accurately feeding back what you are hearing.

Developing these skills will make you far more personally effective. Each requires real commitment to change and a recognition that you will ultimately be a resource for your people.

How else can you bring out a quality performance from your team? Read on!

FOCUS ON RESULTS, NOT REASONS

Your department's productivity slipped sharply last month. The problems were only temporary, but your boss wants a detailed list of reasons for the decline. How do you handle the situation and keep your employees in a good light?

Furnish your boss with a written memo citing the exact causes of the work slippage, along with plans for improvements. Avoid placing blame, especially within your work group.

A focus on reasons puts employees on the defensive, stress Ed Oakley and Doug Krug, authors of *Enlightened Leadership* (Simon & Schuster). Avoid asking your employees:

- Why are you behind schedule?
- Who isn't keeping up?
- Don't you know better than that?
- Who made that decision?

Instead, ask "results" questions:

- What have we accomplished so far that you're most pleased with?
- How do you want our next project to turn out?
- What key things must happen if we're going to reach our objectives?

WHAT IS A QUALITY LEADER?

What characteristics do quality leaders have?

1. They know their own strengths and weaknesses.

2. They make the path smooth so employees can get their jobs done.

3. They are honest and trustworthy and expect the same qualities from their employees.

4. They spend less time on day-to-day activities and more time on communicating.

5. They recognize the value of employees' contributions and let employees known when they've done a good job.

6. They serve as models of good leadership that employees can look up to and respect, and they, in turn, respect their employees.

— AREND "SANDY" SANDBULTE, CEO, MINNESOTA POWER,
IN *INDUSTRY WEEK*

CALL HER *MAJOR* SUPERVISOR

Many of the principles of workplace leadership are based on military guidelines, Patrick L. Townsend and Joan E. Gebhardt note in *Quality in Action* (John Wiley & Sons). Here are some leadership pointers from the U.S. Marine Corps:

1. Take responsibility. Be accountable for your own actions and those of your coworkers. Judgment and tact are vital.

2. Know yourself. Evaluate yourself honestly, and strive to become the best person in your organization.

3. Set an example. Standards of correct behavior are far more influential than disciplinary measures.

4. Have confidence in others. Tell people what to do — but not *how* to do it.

5. Be available. Let others do their own work, but offer guidance when it's needed.

6. Be a provider. Make certain your coworkers get essential help and supplies.

7. Keep everyone informed. Squelch unfounded rumors, and be sure everyone receives the correct information.

8. Set attainable goals. Unrealistic goals create frustration and damage morale. Go after challenging, but reachable, objectives.

9. Make sound and timely decisions. If you've made a bad decision, change it now.

10. Know your job. Keep up with current trends and changes in your line of work.

11. Build teamwork. Train everyone to carry their share of the load, and teach them to understand the value of their contributions.

DON'T KEEP YOUR DISTANCE, COACH!

Conventional advice to new supervisors is, "Keep your distance from your subordinates." But that advice may be creating a barrier to effective supervision, suggest the results of research conducted by Personnel Decisions International (PDI), a Minneapolis consulting firm.

Coaches are more likely to provide effective developmental coaching to people with whom they have formed strong relationships, says the survey. Research participants say the most important factor that creates effective coaching is honest, straightforward communication. And, when coaching fails, it is most often because coaches have *not* taken the time to establish a supportive and trusting relationship with those they coach.

What are some coaching "turn-offs" that you may want to avoid? The research suggests:

- noncaring relationship

- lack of specific feedback

- vague philosophical advice

- irrelevant, unneeded advice

- impersonal, one-way relationship

- negative, critical, or abusive feedback.

The survey information was compiled by conducting in-person and telephone interviews with 30 line managers and executives from a variety of companies. It is part of PDI's ongoing research that studies how people learn and develop at work.

FOUR WAYS TO KICK-START CREATIVITY

An ability to "think out of the box" — to find new solutions to old problems — is a powerful personal quality skill to develop. But it's not always easy to "click into" a creative viewpoint. Here are some ways to stimulate creativity within your work group:

- Encourage creative people to take risks by rewarding efforts and processes, not only results.

- Allow mistakes.

- Support persistence. Not all innovations come from flashes of imagination.

- Maintain a relaxing atmosphere.

— CY CHARNEY,
THE MANAGER'S TOOL KIT (AMACOM)

CREATIVE EMPLOYEES REQUIRE SPECIAL HANDLING

Creativity is the lifeblood of quality improvement. But managing creative employees is sometimes counterintuitive. "It goes against business principles because of the nature of the work and the workers themselves," declares Jeffrey Beir, senior vice president with Lotus Development Corporation, a successful software company that nurtures creativity in its employees.

Creative work — developing a new product from scratch — attracts people who are most often perfectionists, may not use good interpersonal psychology, and may be unaware of their effect on others, generalizes Beir. And, creatives often don't fit into tradition, observes Beir: They are intense and focused on work all of the time. They like to solve puzzles and usually work for the fun of creation, admiration from their peers, and the excitement of creating success. They are not generally interested in corporate politics. "These individuals may not fit into corporate culture, but they are necessary for the corporate destiny," explains Beir.

If you are charged with leading a creative team of engineers, artists, writers, designers, scientists, or others who develop products from the ground up, what tactics work best to supervise them? Beir suggests adopting some approaches that have worked well at Lotus:

1. Select rules carefully. Creatives often fight rules, says Beir. Arbitrary rules constrain creativity in these innovative individuals.

2. Articulate the vision. Be clear about what you want, says Beir. Tell the team, and then trust the creative process to make the vision become reality.

3. Plan with the "slow is fast" method. Take time to plan carefully up front, always focusing on the vision and goals of the project. And anticipate and remove any and all barriers to the creative process.

4. Avoid focusing on back-up plans. Instead of making contingency plans ("what to do, if … "), prepare and develop methods of resolving problems. "Problems are exceptions, not part of the plan," explains Beir.

5. Involve the team; listen. "There is no vice president of ideas," says Beir. Respect what you hear.

6. Manage group dynamics. Since creative people tend to be unaware of their impact on others, group meetings can become chaotic, explains Beir. If possible, keep the teams small, he suggests. And let team members help select new members. "It's good if everyone likes each other."

Even when team members like working together, meetings can get wild, with everyone talking at once. Or they can get off focus because of the threads of ideas that are tossed out. Lotus teams use several group-dynamics tricks to bring them back on target. For example: They pass around the Lotus version of a "talking stick." The person who holds the stick gets to talk uninterrupted. Or, they shout "Rat hole!" when the group gets mired in secondary ideas away from the main focus of their project. And sometimes, to save words, they just give a "thumbs-up" to signal a job well done, instead of piling on praise.

The primary role of a supervisor of creative people? Become a "beekeeper," advises Beir. "Create a beehive in which people and ideas swarm around."

Seven Hidden Reasons for Poor Performance

When faced with poor performance, a lot of supervisors opt to eliminate the employee in question rather than to eliminate the reason behind the performance behavior. Many supervisors wrongly blame poor performance on lack of motivation or on a poor hiring selection by the company, states Ferdinand E. Fournies, author of *Why Employees Don't Do What They're Supposed To Do* (Tab Books).

But, in reality, Fournies claims that the majority of performance problems are caused by poor management — not bad employees. The next time you feel ready to run an employee out the door, make sure you are not the problem. Use the following checklist to identify nonperformance issues:

1. They don't know what to do. Are you paying your employees to guess what you want them to do instead of telling them specifically what you expect? *Solution:* Give employees accurate job descriptions that spell out what you expect. Specify the steps required to accomplish each goal, the dates each step should begin and end, and the results you want.

2. They don't know how to do it. People are often promoted several times without being taught how to do each job. *Solution:* Choose one person to train new employees and provide training and reference manuals. Later, test for training effectiveness.

3. They don't know why they should do it. Many employees don't see the relevance of their work. *Solution:* Explain how their particular jobs benefit the organization.

4. They think their way is better. Many employees assume they were hired to reinvent their jobs. *Solution:* Before work begins, get input from your employees. If someone presents a feasible idea for "working smarter," try it. But if the idea won't work, sell him or her on your idea.

5. They think something else is more important. Some of your employees may have different priorities than you. *Solution:* Prioritize projects as you assign them. Give each employee a list of priority categories to rank assignments themselves.

6. They think they are doing it. Many employees assume that if they are left alone, they're doing a good job. *Solution:* Give positive feedback several times per day. Record achievement rates, and focus feedback on performance — not the person.

7. They are rewarded for not doing it. Sometimes poor performers are given easy assignments instead of being held accountable to work to standard. *Solution:* Monitor difficult tasks closely until performance meets your expectations.

I WISH I'D SAID THAT!

Are you sometimes at a loss for words when you need to give an employee feedback? Here are two examples of feedback — one poor and one good:

Poor: "Joe, you aren't welding that seam right. Fix it."

Good: "Joe, let me show you where you didn't meet the specifications on this seam weld. And then we'll talk about how you can practice to meet the specifications."

The second example is good because the employee hears the negative feedback as a way to improve performance, say Seth N. Leibler and Ann W. Parkman in *Workforce Training News.*

Key point: Good feedback helps employees believe in their ability to do the work.

'No Fault' Firing Can Ease Termination Jitters

Regardless of how much "seasoning" a supervisor has acquired, terminating an employee — even when firing is justified because of nonperformance — is an unnerving experience. And the task doesn't get easier when the only reason for the termination is downsizing or "rightsizing."

"In many cases, those about to be eliminated are good employees who may have survived previous cutbacks and even taken on extra work without a raise or promotion," says William Ayers, president of The Ayers Group Inc., an outplacement and recruiting firm based in New York. "Telling this individual that he or she is being eliminated must be done in a systematic, but compassionate, manner."

Ayers recommends a process he calls "no-fault termination," a firing method that keeps communication clear, buffers the worker from unnecessary emotional stress, helps reduce anger, and protects the company from potential legal problems.

"We teach supervisors that the termination is not the fault of the individual employee, nor the person doing the terminating, nor the company. This is the professional way in today's economic climate to fire workers who have performed well. The employees' efforts then can be focused on looking ahead to finding a new position. But, if you insult a person and don't allow his or her dignity to remain intact ... the natural reaction is to hurt back. Most people don't turn the other cheek."

Supervisors sometimes fall into termination traps: They give performance appraisals, rehash past grievances, and sometimes side with the fired employee by suggesting that the company is at fault.

But when they use no-fault termination methods, they deliver the news compassionately. Here are the suggested steps of this type of termination procedure:

- **Get to the bad news fast.** Exchange pleasantries, but avoid nervous chatter — delaying only makes matters worse.

- **Focus on the task.** Talking about the "good old days" may ease your conscience, but it's counterproductive for the person who needs to look ahead.

- **Don't be a "hit-and-run" terminator.** After delivering the news, personally escort the worker to the next step — usually the human resources department for details on a termination package. Treat the employee with dignity throughout this process.

- **Avoid airing your own frustrations about the firing.** And don't say, "I know how you feel." You can't — know you still have a job.

- **Make the termination a clean break.** Don't suggest alternatives, like transfers and demotions, if they are out of the question.

- **Remain calm.** Keep your cool, even if the employee blows up.

- **Involve security.** If the employee appears to be a danger to himself or herself or to coworkers, call for security or arrange for a referral to your company's employee-assistance program (EAP). Inform your human resources staff and other pertinent workers of your concerns.

- **Remember that you're not the bad guy.** Like hiring, firing is an unavoidable part of your job. "Firing people is a delicate skill that few supervisors ever formally learn," says Ayers.

"With the increased incidence of violence in the workplace, companies are trying different strategies to provide education for supervisors on the do's and don'ts of letting good people go. No-fault termination training should be provided right before a staff reduction is announced."

"A company," adds Ayers, "shows its true colors when it hires, fires, and relocates [employees]. That's why it is important to practice the 'right way' to do things."

SPRUCE UP YOUR APPRAISALS

Traditional performance-appraisal processes fall short of improving performance, states says Rick Maurer, author of *Feedback Tool Kit* (Productivity Press). The reason: They "attach grades," promote one-way discussions, and put a judge's robes on supervisors. And these things get in the way of actually overcoming barriers to improving work.

Despite the shortcomings of performance appraisals, however, employees are hungry for helpful feedback. "Most discussions about performance are sugar-coated or watered down. Not only do supervisors tend not to criticize — for fear of saying the wrong thing and making matters worse — they do not praise their people. So, bad performers aren't aware of what they are doing wrong, and good performers don't know they are achieving," observes Maurer.

Maurer recommends a change from the traditional annual performance appraisal: Replace it with an annual planning session that promotes a two-way discussion between supervisors and workers and establishes an ongoing dialogue of job feedback. "Most supervisors have the skills to conduct effective performance appraisals, but they need to trust themselves more and apply those skills," says Maurer. He gives six tips to help supervisors in a formal feedback process:

1. Prepare. "Do your homework in advance of any discussion and provide examples of what your workers are doing well and what they need to improve on. You also need to support yourself by reviewing notes prior to a meeting, rehearsing if you believe it will be a particularly tough session, and allowing yourself a few minutes prior to the meeting to clear your mind and focus on the session," he explains.

2. Present. Maurer suggests focusing on a few key points during the feedback session. "Keep it simple, make your point, give an example or two, and move on to the next point. But don't give tons of examples. People can get overwhelmed and overloaded and don't hear you anymore." And if you focus your remarks on what customers say and desire, you'll find that your employees can "take" stronger feedback, observes Maurer.

3. Listen. "Once you have made your points, stop talking and make sure your employees understand what you have said. You might ask them to paraphrase your comments. Ask if they have any questions. People can only take in so much, so pace yourself between presenting information and listening to responses," he suggests.

4. Encourage dialogue. Ask your employees about their long-range goals, and volunteer how you can help in their career development.

5. Develop an action plan. Performance improvement is a joint venture between the supervisor and the employee, says Maurer. The supervisor's role is to provide the right environment and tools for the job to be successfully accomplished.

6. Acknowledge the employee. "Thank your employees for participating in the discussion, providing input, and making a commitment to improve their work and the work of the department. Acknowledge that it was a tough meeting and that you are glad they stuck with it," suggests Maurer.

To reinforce these points and further encourage feedback,

Maurer advises supervisors to hold project debriefing sessions with the entire work group at critical points in project work. "This allows for discussion of what is working and what changes are necessary."

Supervisors should "wander around" and make themselves accessible for feedback on a day-to-day basis. "You don't need to have an agenda. Just be visible and available for dialogue with your workers."

IDEA IN ACTION

DISCOVER HOW EMPLOYEES RATE YOU

How am I doing? Your employees probably ask you this question frequently. But do you ever ask *them* how *you* are doing?

At Amoco Corp., supervisors ask. And they get told. The asking and telling are parts of Amoco's upward-appraisal process, in which subordinates give feedback to supervisors on their leadership and management skills. "It has been quite a cultural change," says Bernie Siebenaler, director of Amoco's performance-management system. "Initially, it's tough for managers to go through, but, in the long run, we think it will help them to improve their leadership skills."

Upward appraisals are similar to attitude surveys (in each, feedback is almost always anonymous), but the two feedback instruments differ significantly, explains Siebenaler. Surveys deal with broader organizational and cultural issues, and upward appraisals are designed to give specific feedback to individual supervisors about their management behaviors and styles.

Amoco employees complete appraisals on their supervisors. Then the supervisors share the appraisal information with a facilitator (someone from human resources or an outside consultant). They review the data and identify themes — such as a tendency to become too involved in daily activities.

A team meeting between the supervisor, the employees, and the facilitator is the next step. "The purpose of the team meeting is to share the survey results and to create a developmental action plan," says Siebenaler. Then the supervisor is given time and the resources (such as training) to make improvements in supervisory effectiveness. The supervisor also reviews the action plan with his or her own boss and incorporates these actions into the performance-management cycle.

Amoco intends to use this upward-appraisal process with all of its supervisors — about 6,000 individuals, says Siebenaler.

What kinds of questions are included on an upward appraisal? Here are samples:

- Does your supervisor have a clear vision of the work group's role in supporting the overall company goal?

- Does your supervisor stay on top of emerging trends in the industry and identify areas for growth?

- Is your supervisor creating a process for developing quality rather than checking quality after the work is completed?

- Does your supervisor coach individuals for improved performance?

- Does your supervisor give public credit for the employee's success, or only criticize mistakes?

If those questions were asked of you, how would your employees rate *your* performance?

TUNE IN TO EFFECTIVE TRAINING VIDEOS

Training videos can be an effective tool in helping your team boost quality. But be careful: All training videos are not created equally. Here are some tips on selecting a training video from Connie Sasseen Bever, of American Media, Inc., a West Des Moines, Iowa, training-video producer. She advises choosing videos that are:

- **Targeted.** Before you begin evaluating videos, define the objectives of the training program. Check all videos you preview to see if they target and support these objectives.

- **Appropriate and realistic.** The video should depict a work environment and situation appropriate for your employees, and the characters and issues should be realistic.

- **Informative.** Any video you select should have a good balance of teaching and entertaining. Too much of either is an ineffective use of time.

- **Interesting.** The movie should be interesting and well-paced, and should command attention.

- **Representative.** Characters should represent a diverse and realistic workforce.

- **Logical.** The content of the video should be presented logically and should be easy to follow.

- **Current.** Look for outmoded language, clothing, hair styles, or office furniture, says Bever. Even though these "trimmings" are irrelevant, viewers can get hung up on them and overlook the message of the movie.

In addition to these checkpoints, make sure the video is the right length for your employees — usually not more than 22 minutes, suggests Bever. Finally, check out the leader's guide and support materials. They should reinforce the key points of the video.

QUICK TIPS

- **Use silence to make a point.** Saying the right thing at the right time can have a tremendous impact in a meeting with your employees. But don't forget that silence can be a powerful communicator. A well-placed pause can emphasize an important point or encourage others to contribute their ideas.

- **Give credit where credit is due.** End your departmental meetings by summarizing tasks and contributions. And, whenever possible, attribute ideas to individuals, such as by saying, "As Marianne suggested, we will ... "

- **Watch your wording.** Show employees that you're working together as a team. You'll find you'll get better results by saying, "Let's talk about how we can ... " instead of saying, "You're going to have to ... "

- **Keep irate employees calm.** If you have to deal with an irate employee, talk calmly and use the individual's name often. People are naturally comforted by the sound of their own name, advises Kelly Tyler, a trainer for Keye Productivity Center.

- **Avoid red ink.** Leave the red pen in your desk when you review or edit reports by your employees or coworkers. Red ink evokes unsavory memories of high school English class for many people. Choose a blue or green pen to make your suggestions.

- **Gain job applicant insights.** When you interview job applicants, ask: "What's the most rewarding workday you've had this year? Why?" Their answers can give you helpful insights into what really motivates prospective employees.

- **Project leadership.** Act like the leader that you are, even when you are a meeting participant. Sit up straight and lean forward slightly. Use good eye contact. And if you are interrupted, quietly, but confidently, assert yourself to regain the floor.

- **Uncover cost cutters.** Ask every new hire to come up with three cost-cutting ideas. New workers, especially those from other companies or industries, bring new perspectives to your organization. "Old" ideas from their former companies may be new to you.

HOW TO BE 'THE BEST' BOSS

"To get a quality performance from my team, I think it's important that my employees respect me. But it's also important to me that they know I care about them as people. Is it possible to be friends with employees and still gain their respect?"

— P.N., Sioux City, Iowa

Successful supervisors walk a fine line between being friendly and losing authority with their employees. They communicate their expectations, then give feedback and recognition to build understanding and trust. Their consistent behavior results in a motivated workforce that has confidence in its leader.

Have you developed the traits that employees value in their bosses? Assess yourself by writing Yes or No after each question, then score yourself below.

1. Have you developed a "sixth sense" that tells you when employees are unhappy with their jobs or with you? _____

2. Are you able to strike a happy balance between being too distant and too involved with employees? _____

3. Do you know what new bosses should do to gain employee trust, especially if they have been promoted from within the organization? _____

4. Do you avoid interpersonal mistakes that supervisors sometimes make which demotivate employees? _____

5. Do you focus on the problem, not the person, when correcting employees? _____

6. Are you adept at admitting your mistakes without losing your credibility? _____

7. Are you able to make a satisfactory response when a higher-up complains about your employees? _____

8. Do you know why being predictable is vital to your effectiveness? _____

9. Do you know how to answer employees who don't agree with upper-management decisions — when you don't either? _____

10. Do you know how to show employees that their ideas are valued even when they aren't adopted? _____

ARE YOU A GOOD SUPERVISOR? Add up the total number of Yes answers. A score of 9 or 10 suggests that you are doing a great job of gaining respect from employees and maintaining their friendship. A score of eight is average; a score of seven or less suggests there are still ways you can encourage quality work from your work team without losing their friendship and respect.

Your Quality Take-Away

Supervising for a Quality Performance
What *You* Can Do

As a supervisor, you have a major responsibility for helping an organization's quality effort succeed. When a quality program is put into place, it's up to you to sell employees on its importance and to encourage a top-notch performance from them.

- Before placing blame for a defect or error on an employee, make certain that employees have adequate equipment, materials, supplies, and instruction.

- Be sure you know how to utilize videos and other training opportunities to make employees understand quality and their role in achieving it.

- You need to be able to walk that fine line of being liked *and* respected.

- You must understand how to conduct fair appraisals, and how to terminate an employee when it becomes necessary to do so.

A successful supervisor understands people. You must know how to encourage cooperation from difficult workers while encouraging creativity from the gifted members of the staff. The many facets of supervising strengthen a range of skills that build a sturdy foundation for a long career in leadership roles.

CHAPTER NINE

Creating Quality Frontline Customer Service

"Customers come C.O.D. — through Communication,
Observation, and Dedication."

— Zig Ziglar,
AUTHOR AND MOTIVATIONAL SPEAKER

INTRODUCTION

Prior to the early 1980s, most literature about quality focused on the physical product. "Service" quality was a byproduct of marketing, something that either helped the customer choose a product or use it later. Service was something extra — having to do with such things as payment terms, directions for use, guarantees, repairs, maintenance, and other "nonhuman" issues.

Today, you can page through scores of books about quality and you won't find even one that *doesn't* define quality in terms of customers and customer satisfaction. And that makes sense. A process, product, or service has no relevance without customers; everything that's done in an organization is done for the customer. Attracting, serving, and retaining customers is the ultimate purpose of any company. Without a customer focus, a commitment to quality is meaningless.

As a customer service representative, you play a pivotal role in your company's commitment to quality and excellence. You are on the front line, dealing with the client. You report the bad — as well as the good — to the people who can change or improve your product or service. There are a few things that you can do to help your firm achieve better quality of materials and services:

1. Listen to clients. Spend the time daily to discover your clients' wants, desires, frustrations, and successes. Know how they use your products or services in specific detail. Knowing them better will help you serve them better.

2. Ask questions. Don't let a quietly simmering problem boil over from lack of attention. Learn to ask your clients effective questions about the performance of your products and services. Write down what they tell you.

3. Report findings. Immediately and completely share the information about your client with those who can bring about change. A small alteration, such as changing a service schedule or modifying product design, can vastly improve what you offer to customers. It might even make the difference between buying from you or a competitor.

4. Notify clients. If your company affects a change (and policy permits), call the client back to let him or her know what's been done. Not only will your customer know you've really listened, but he or she will also have a sense of partnership with your company's quality and excellence. If your client realizes that your firm constantly strives to improve, he or she will keep coming back, and everyone benefits. But you can achieve this only through effective, regular communication with your clients and management.

Customer service is the quality hot seat. You are the link between your company and its customers. Your actions can make or break the relationship between your organization and the customer. How can you provide the quality customer service that customers expect? Here are some ideas.

PRACTICE WHAT YOU PROMISE

Late in the day, a customer places an order that she needs "right now." You may lose the order if you don't promise overnight delivery — a promise you aren't sure you can keep.

You obviously want to do all you can to provide quality service, but if you can't keep a promise, you'll do more harm to your company's reputation — and your own — than you'll do good. Saying "Sorry, but I can't promise that" may be difficult, but it's much easier than saying "Sorry the order didn't get to you when I said it would."

When a customer (internal or external) asks for a promise:

- **Know what is impossible.** Promises get us in trouble when we don't know all the facts. If you aren't sure, find out before you commit yourself.

- **Don't bow to pressure.** When a customer, coworker, or boss is in a hurry, you may not have time to think of all the consequences. But don't just tell people what they want to hear. The truth is better than broken pledges.

- **Keep your promises.** If you do give your word, you'd better follow through. You'll gain a reputation as someone to be trusted.

'QUALITY? I KNOW IT WHEN I SEE IT'

Quality. "It's a nice word and all, but what does it mean?" a frustrated customer service rep asked recently as she sipped coffee from her "Quality" coffee mug. Ken Blanchard, author of *The One-Minute Manager* (William Morrow) and professor of leadership and organizational behavior at the University of Massachusetts at Amherst, says many managers and supervisors talk about the need for quality without explaining what it is and how it can be achieved.

Ask a customer what makes quality in a product or service, and the reply might be, "It's hard for me to describe it, but I know it when I see it." What the customer is saying is that quality is something that is perceived, or felt, as well as seen.

A recent Gallup Poll asked 1,005 adults to measure "quality" in the companies they do business with. The top factors they cited were: courteous or polite behavior, satisfied needs, promptness, and a satisfying past experience with the company.

Quality, ultimately, is what the customer expects to receive and is satisfied with when that expectation is met. "Quality is more than an attribute; quality is an attitude," says the narrator in the film *The Human Nature of Quality* (Dartnell).

Set your own quality goals. Forget the clichés and vague motivational posters. You can help bring meaning to your company's quality goals through your personal definition of quality. What follows are goals for customer service excellence that you may want to adopt for yourself.

Each day, promise yourself:

1. To always maintain a professional manner and appearance.

2. To greet customers warmly on the telephone and to always make them feel welcome and comfortable doing business with you and your organization.

3. To always be prompt, courteous, and friendly in serving customers.

4. To always adopt a problem-solving attitude when you handle complaints and inquiries.

5. To carefully assess each customer's needs and recommend specific products or services that will provide the highest level of satisfaction.

6. To find the right answers to all customer questions and to keep up-to-date on the products and services your company offers so you can pass the correct information on to your customers.

7. To be familiar with all organizational procedures and policies so you can handle every customer transaction with minimum error and delay.

8. To follow up on inquiries from customers and ensure their satisfaction.

9. To know your company's promotional campaigns and to support these efforts whenever you deal with customers.

10. To turn new customers into returning customers by providing the kind of service they expect and are entitled to.

CREATING LEGENDARY SERVICE

Businesses spend a lot of time, energy, and money finding new customers. They advertise, carry out surveys, hand out coupons and discounts, and practically do headstands to generate new business. In the shuffle, it's easy to forget a company's most important customer — the one that's on the phone right now.

The fact is, it costs businesses six times more to gain a new customer than to retain a current one. And customers who do business with you again and again generally increase their purchases steadily over the years. The bottom line is this: Each time you provide top-notch customer service to a current customer, you're helping ensure your company's success well into the future.

Here are tips from four experts to help you create legendary customer service — the kind of service that keeps your customers coming back:

Tip #1: Make customers feel important. "The more important you make customers feel, the better they will feel about doing business with you," says Richard E. Gerson, Ph.D., author of *Beyond Customer Service* (Crisp Publications). "Call them by name, ask them to tell you about themselves, and ask questions about their accomplishments. Your reward will be a lifetime customer."

Tip #2: Exceed expectations. "There is no more powerful way to keep customers than to exceed their expectations," says consultant Paul R. Timm. "It's a process I call E-Plus. It means first, strive to sharpen your understanding of what customers want and expect from you. Then two: Constantly look for ways to give customers more than they expect. Provide it faster. Offer to deliver it. A well-known air freight company claims to deliver your package by 10 a.m. the next morning, but often delivers it by 9:00 or 9:30. That's the service customers remember."

Tip #3: Use your radar. You represent one of your company's most valuable means of gauging whether current customers are happy. "Think of yourself as a sort of frontline radar, an early warning system," says management consultant Karl Albrecht in *The Service Advantage* (Dow Jones-Irwin Books). Encourage customers to speak up about what's wrong (and right) about the service they receive from your company. "Ask a few well-placed questions," suggests Albrecht, such as, "Were you satisfied with your shopping experience with us this morning?" "Is there any message you'd like me to pass on to our manager for you?" and "Was there anything we could have done better in serving you today?" Such questions will not only help correct an existing problem, but you'll also be showing the customer just how much you value his or her opinion.

Tip #4: Do more listening. "There's probably no better way to persuade your customers — to get them to believe you, have confidence in you, and buy from you — than to truly listen to them," says Ron Willingham, author of *Hey, I'm the Customer!* (Prentice Hall). "When you listen, you silently say to your customers, 'I want to understand you; I want to understand your needs or wants. I want to solve your problems because you're important. When you're happy and satisfied, you'll come back and tell others. Then I'll be more successful.'"

CUSTOMER RELATIONSHIPS FORMED IN 7 SECONDS

Your first contact with a customer will determine how he or she feels about you, your products or services, and your entire organization. And, it takes only seven seconds.

Whether it's in-person or on the telephone, customers form 11 impressions during that tiny slice of time, claims Ron Willingham, author of *Hey, I'm the Customer!* (Prentice Hall). "Most of us form quick first impressions," Willingham says. "We often subliminally decide whether we like people, feel good about them, or want to do business with them in those first few seconds of contact. It all happens on unconscious, intuitive, and instinctive levels."

Willingham, who is chairman of Integrity Training Systems in Phoenix, says there are three specific actions reps can take to create a winning impression during those first few moments of contact with customers. His advice:

1. Get "eye contact." You don't have to be serving a customer face-to-face to make the kind of "eye contact" Willingham is referring to. As an example, he cites his own experience calling his local telephone company when he needed extra phone lines installed in his office.

"In the past, when attempting to deal with the phone company, I usually was handled in a disinterested, controlled way. This time was totally different. I could feel that telephone company representative looking directly into my eyes, even over the telephone," Willingham says.

"She was totally plugged into me, despite the limitations over a telephone line. We couldn't have had more rapport if we had been face-to-face. She was completely focused on me and tuned in to my wavelength. I had the feeling that she caught every nuance of my voice, attitude, pacing, and emotional tone." For example, the moment the rep detected she could joke with Willingham, she did. She knew how far she could carry it all within good business taste. "That's what people skilled in communications effectiveness do. They listen to people's emotions, pace, tone, and attitudes."

2. Thank customers for coming in, contacting you, or seeing you. "That's not what the receptionist did the last time I went into the dental office," recalls Willingham. "I stood at the counter at least a full minute that seemed more like ten. Finally she looked up, showed no reaction to me — no smile, no warmth, no nothing — and said, 'Sign in!' I'd been going to that office for over 35 years. Frankly, I was accustomed to being fussed over when I walked in that door."

His advice: Whether it's the customer's first or 50th visit, "fuss" over him or her. Let the customer know just how important he or she is to you and your organization.

3. Tune the world out and them in. Effective customer service reps "Break preoccupation. They notice people. Really notice them," Willingham says. In his seminars, he tells customer service reps that the best way to improve the service they provide is by observing the service they get from others. "Go out and do your own research," he says. "Check out places where you spend money. See how little common courtesies are done — or not done — by others. Notice how great you feel when someone greets you properly. Notice how you feel when people say with their actions, 'Hey, you're the customer ... you pay my salary!'"

Says Willingham: "Your own research will show you just what you need to do to make others feel happy they've done business with you. Put those lessons to work for you the next time you pick up the telephone."

Being Responsive Is Only a Start

In the minds of business professionals, quality is usually associated with results. However, this may not always be the case for your customers. Customers often view service — how they are treated — as the measure of quality, say the authors of *Bringing TQM on the QT to Your Organization* (SPC Press, Inc.). Something as simple as turnaround time on callbacks can quickly establish a customer's impression of your company's commitment to quality.

"Being responsive is the bare minimum," say the authors. "It's nothing close to total quality, but it's a start."

Let's Do This Again (and Again!)

The easiest customer to satisfy is the one you already have. Your competitors have to work extra hard to take customers away if you do what you're supposed to do. But, as soon as you start to neglect current customers, you make it easy for competitors to sneak in. Here are some ways to satisfy current customers again and again:

- **Call to wish customers a happy birthday.** Or perhaps you'd rather recognize their anniversary with your company. Whatever milestone you choose to celebrate, make it a purely social call. Don't let customers wonder what you really called about. Keep all business out of the conversation, and you'll show your customers that you value them as people, not just as account numbers.

- **Drop by to say 'Hello.'** If you really happen to be in the neighborhood of a longtime customer, stop in to say

"Hello." State from the start the informal purpose of your call and the short amount of time you intend to take. You don't want to interrupt a busy day, so be sensitive to the customer's schedule.

- **Identify discounts or other savings.** Customers appreciate when you have their best interests — not just their business — at heart. Demonstrate your concern by alerting them when items they usually purchase go on sale, or if they could save money by altering their purchasing schedule.

- **Study the big picture.** Don't look at each customer interaction as an isolated event, but as part of a larger relationship. Determine what is best for the customer — not just today, but a year from now. If possible, sit down and plan out your service with long-term customers to show the depth of your commitment.

NEED FAST-ON-YOUR-FEET SOLUTIONS? TRY THESE

Many customer-related problems on the telephone can be avoided with a quick, appropriate response from you. Here are some minor problems that may arise — and "fast-on-your feet" responses that you can make to prevent a problem from escalating:

- **Problem:** A caller hasn't given his name and declines to do so after your request.

  What to do: Let the caller know why you need his name. Say, "Having your name would make it possible to ..."

- **Problem:** The customer's speech is garbled, and you simply do not understand what she just said.

What to do: You don't want to insult the customer for being inarticulate, so you must be particularly careful. Start by saying, "I'm having a hard time understanding you, Ms. Smith. Could you please speak more slowly?" If that doesn't work, say, "Let me be sure I heard you correctly. Were you saying that ... ?" and then repeat what you think the caller said.

- **Problem:** A coworker begins talking to you, and you've become distracted, missing what your caller has just said.

  What to do: Be honest: "I'm sorry, Mr. Jackson. I was distracted for a moment. Could you please repeat what you just said?" Or say, "I'm not sure I understand you clearly. Could you please restate your request?"

- **Problem:** The caller isn't speaking loudly enough.

  What to do: Say, "We don't have a great connection, Mrs. Brown. Could you speak a little more loudly?" Or say, "We've got some background noises here that make it hard for me to hear. Would you mind speaking a little louder?"

- **Problem:** It's early morning, and the person the customer wants to talk to has not yet arrived.

  What to do: Since it's early and your coworker isn't expected in yet, you don't have to worry about "covering" for him or her. Tell the caller the truth: "Mr. Kaplan hasn't arrived yet. I'd be happy to tell him you called." Then find out if it is necessary for the caller to speak only to Mr. Kaplan. Ask, "Is there something I can help you with?"

- **Problem:** It's early afternoon, and the customer asks for someone who has already left to attend to personal business.

What to do: Don't explain too much. Say, "Mary Smith is not in this afternoon. I can take your message and see that she receives it first thing tomorrow morning."

- **Problem:** Your boss wants you to screen her calls.

  What to do: Ask callers, "May I tell Ms. Williams who's calling, please?" or say, "Ms. Williams is in a private conference at the moment. As soon as she's available, I'll see that she receives your message."

- **Problem:** The caller asks for information that is available from another department but starts explaining the problem to you.

  What to do: Say, "Mrs. Stacy in our accounting department is the person who would be able to help you most effectively. I'd be happy to transfer your call." Or say, "Thank you for explaining your concern. Mrs. Stacy in our accounting department is better prepared to help you in that area. I'd be happy to transfer you."

The Pros Know:
Tips from Service Reps

Looking for some ideas on how to improve your telephone customer service skills? Consider these bits of advice from some real expert front-line customer service reps.

- **Good service and a weather report!** Customer service representative Beverly Stark has found a unique way to personalize the calls she receives at Graphic Controls Corporation in Buffalo, New York. Before leaving for work each morning, Stark watches The Weather Channel, observing the different weather patterns across the United States and paying particular attention to any troublesome weather conditions. Then, when she is on the telephone with customers, she refers to the weather they're experiencing in their respective areas. Says her supervisor, Chris Keye: "Customers appreciate this personal approach and truly feel that our company cares about the customer."

- **Get that name right!** Wendy Neuman, a customer service rep for American Family Life Assurance Company in Columbus, Georgia, knows how important it is to pronounce the customer's name correctly. If she mispronounces a name and the customer corrects her, Neuman makes a special effort to repeat the name (pronounced correctly!) immediately after she's been corrected. She also repeats it several times throughout the call. "I believe this lets the caller know I care about getting their name right," Neuman says.

- **Surprise! A real voice!** At Ritchie Engineering Co., Inc., in Bloomington, Minnesota, it's okay to have callers leave a voice-mail message — but only after hours. "We find our customers much prefer the personal touch — talking to someone who can help them instead of to a machine," says customer service representative Myrtle Mohr. During business hours, all incoming calls are answered personally by a customer service rep, Mohr explains: "If we cannot answer the caller's question, we transfer the call to someone who can."

- **Help! Our switchboard operator has switched off!** Before going on vacation, reps who work at switchboards should compile an instruction sheet for the people who will be substituting for them, suggests Sue Milne, a receptionist at Prairie States Life Insurance Company in Rapid City, South Dakota. The guidelines should include specific forwarding instructions provided by various departments. That way the replacements will be able to answer questions like: What calls will the vice president accept directly? Which calls should first be routed to the secretary or assistant? "Last, but not least, notify each department before going on vacation," Milne advises. "This gives employees the opportunity to fore-warn the new person if an unusual situation is pending."

- **You got that write!** At the Minnesota Valley Electric Cooperative, every phone rep makes a written record of every call that comes into the office. "We note the time of the call, the customer's account number, and a brief description of what transpired," explains Marilyn Landela, a customer service rep. Reps turn their logs over to their supervisor, who can then give her manager and the board of directors accurate and detailed infor-mation about the amount and kinds of calls that were received. The reps don't even mind the extra paperwork, says Landela: "Many times, these logs prove invaluable in tracing problem histories."

NORDSTROM EMPLOYEES ARE 'TRAINED FROM BIRTH'

If you've ever shopped at a Nordstrom department store, you may not remember just what you bought, but you most like-ly remember the service you received. This Seattle-based com-pany is known for its friendly salespeople, exceptional customer service, and unbelievable return policy (every returned item is accepted unquestioned whether you have a sales receipt or not, and whether you've owned it for one week or one year). The only restriction applies to special-occasion dresses. "We used to take them back without tags or receipts, but found that some customers were wearing them once to a party and then return-ing them," says Cheryl Engstrom, Nordstrom's media relations manager.

But, aside from the policies that make shopping here a treat, the salespeople seem genuinely happy and motivated. "We hire happy, friendly, ambitious people from the start, so we see no need for a formal sales training program," says Engstrom. "Our employees are essentially trained in human relations by their parents and learn through mentoring once they get to us."

In addition, Nordstrom keeps employees happy by treating them with respect and giving them the freedom they need to do a good job. Some specifics:

- **Free to roam.** No employee is restricted to showing merchandise only in their particular department. "Many times, our customers are surprised when the salesperson that is helping them pick out a blazer runs them downstairs to get a matching blouse and then offers to help them pick out shoes," says Engstrom. "But we give our salespeople the freedom and authority to stay with a customer throughout that person's shopping experience at Nordstrom," she explains. "We also have personal shoppers if customers want wardrobe consultation and advice."

- **Buck stops here.** Every salesperson is given the greatest possible authority so that customers aren't passed around or made to wait. "It is very rare that a salesperson has to get a manager's approval," says Engstrom. "So most customers are assured of prompt service — no matter what their needs."

- **Regional control.** Although Nordstrom is a national company, it is decentralized. "The buying, operations, and advertising all happen at the regional level, with support from us here in the Seattle office," she explains. "This gives the ownership for success or failure to the region."

- **A "promote from within" policy.** "Every employee on the operations side of Nordstrom has worked the sales floor at some time," says Engstrom. "We never hire from outside above the sales level, so our employees know that they will be in the pool we choose from for promotion," she explains. "For employees who are willing to relocate, the opportunities are endless."

- **Best of the best.** "We select an 'All-Star' from each store every year. It's tough to become one, so it's a big deal. Recipients of this award get a cash bonus as well as an enhanced discount for one year," Engstrom says. "It also makes a big difference at promotion time because the All-Stars are looked at first."

"All of these things work together to give our salespeople the feeling that they have the authority to control their own income and outcome," she says. "You can't eliminate one part of the program and still get the same results. It's these things together that make up the Nordstrom culture."

OOPS! DID I REALLY SAY THAT?

What you say to customers — and how you say it — can have a significant impact on your company's public image. Far too often and far too easily, that image can be a negative one when we don't think before we speak to customers.

"We all know what it's like to misspeak by saying something off the top of our heads," observes Kristin Anderson, co-author with Ron Zemke of *Knock Your Socks Off Answers: Solving Customer Nightmares & Soothing Nightmare Customers* (AMA-COM). "To avoid miscommunications that can escalate into sarcasm, argument, and/or bad feelings, you need to be aware of how your words may be misinterpreted by your customers," Anderson says.

She offers these tips for avoiding such miscommunication:

- List standard questions you ask customers. Then review the questions to make sure they really ask what you intend to say. Rewrite any questions that could be misinterpreted.

- Keep a record of the wild things customers say to you — and you say to them. This list will serve as a reminder of how easy it is for both you and your customers to say the wrong thing. It also may help you to be more cautious verbally, and to forgive your customers for their blunders. "For example," says Anderson, "a bank teller told us about a customer who said, 'I'm trying to balance my checkbook. Can you tell me which checks I wrote that haven't cleared yet?'

  "Service people sometimes say equally outrageous things. A friend of ours once said to a customer, 'Mrs. Duck (her real name), you can just waddle on back there and see Mary.' Thankfully, the customer either hadn't heard or pretended she hadn't."

- Identify your own pet peeves as a customer. Then, follow the golden rule by avoiding imposing these peeves on your customers. One thing that gripes Anderson most is employees who ask, "How may I help you?" but have no intention of actually helping. "After prompting me to start describing my problem or needs, it really irritates me when they say, 'Please hold, and I'll transfer you to ...'" she notes. "This interruption sets the potential for a very negative encounter. I now have an edge in my voice when I talk with the person to whom I've been transferred." Instead, ask, "How may I direct your call?"

- Post your best "verbal goof-up graffiti." Nothing can get you through a tough day better than laughing at yourself. Reading the incredible things that have been said can give you a real lift — as well as remind you how easy it can be to go astray from quality communication.

Recapturing Customer Loyalty

Customer loyalty can never be taken for granted, particularly when a mistake on your company's part has damaged a formerly good relationship. "That's when you need excellent 'recovery skills' that will help recapture the customer's goodwill," says Lisa Ford, president of The Ford Group, Inc., of Atlanta, Georgia.

When a mistake is made, Ford advises, "apologize sincerely. This sounds so basic, but I hear a lot of complaints about apologies that aren't really apologies," Ford says. "Your voice, facial expression, and eye contact should show that you really regret the customer's difficulties."

Use these steps to recapture the customer's loyalty:

1. Fix the problem, not the blame. "Customers are only concerned with having the problem fixed," Ford emphasizes. "They're not interested in who did what, or why it happened. They want action that will put things right."

2. Use extras to compensate for the inconvenience. "Just fixing the problem isn't enough to win back the trust and loyalty of the customer," Ford says. "The way the customer looks at it, things should have been done right the first time around. And because they weren't, the customer has spent time, energy, and perhaps even money dealing with the problem."

Your company may offer compensation as a matter of policy. Ford cites a dental office that offers movie passes, or $10.00 off the bill, for clients who have had to wait for their appointments. (Follow any such policy with enthusiasm, however. Don't be like the tellers at one bank, who sparked a flurry of new service complaints by only very grudgingly handing out the $5 bills promised to all customers who had to wait in line longer than five minutes.)

Even if your company doesn't provide such compensation, Ford says, you can help make amends for the customer's inconvenience. Call the customer about a week after the problem has been resolved. Repeat your apology for the inconvenience, ask if the customer is satisfied, and thank him or her for allowing you to solve the problem. Follow up this call with a handwritten note thanking the customer for his or her patience. Invite the customer to contact you personally with any questions or concerns.

3. Always ask for repeat business. "Be very direct about this," Ford advises. "When you call the customer to see if he or she is satisfied with the resolution, you could end by saying, 'We hope you'll continue to do business with us. Based on how we handled this problem, will you?'"

4. Initiate problem prevention. "Be proactive in suggesting changes that you think will avert the kinds of problems or concerns that damage customer loyalty," Ford urges. "Look for problems you can solve. Let's say you've taken a few calls from customers who are confused about an item in your company's mail order catalog. They've ordered the merchandise, only to discover that the color was not as depicted in the catalog. Track these calls, and notify the appropriate person: 'Perhaps we need to alter the description to depict this item more accurately in the catalog.'"

CASHING IN ON CUSTOMER FEEDBACK

How are you doing? Are you increasing your knowledge, improving your personal image, advancing your career? Or are you spinning your wheels? According to Plato, "The life that is unexamined is not worth living." How true! Self-assessment is the key to self-improvement.

If you are employed in sales or as a customer service representative, self-assessment from a career and job standpoint is inextricably tied to the critical question: How do your customers feel about the products and service they are getting?

Examining and evaluating yourself is well and good. But unless your personal evaluation matches your customers' assessment, your self-appraisal may be falling short of the mark. How you are doing — plus how your comp any and its products and service are doing — depends in large measure on the quality of your performance from your customers' point of view.

The conclusion is clear: To assess yourself intelligently and practically you will need information that helps you zero in accurately on the efficiency and profit value of your products, services, and customer treatment as they are perceived by your customers. The best way to determine the level of customer satisfaction in response to your efforts is by obtaining and cashing in on customer feedback. Feedback can be communicated either aggressively or passively.

To pursue feedback aggressively, question the customer directly:

"Was the problem resolved to your complete satisfaction?"

"Do you have any complaints about the product or service?"

"Is there anything about the transaction you would like me to clarify?"

"Do you have any reservations about the way it was handled?"

Passive feedback is the kind that comes to you *gratis* and can be equally, if not more, enlightening. A customer complaint, for example, can be a valuable input for service and sales personnel — an indication that something is amiss that requires attention.

Not all customers readily voice their gripes, and this may

cause the problem to fester. Customers who keep their complaints to themselves are often well on the way to becoming ex-customers. This underlines the importance of passive feedback as demonstrated, for example, by the customer's changed behavior:

- An unaccustomed coolness or aloofness;

- A decline in orders or calls;

- A lack of interest in new products or special offers, reflected in the look in the customer's eyes or in the sound of his or her voice.

All you have to do is to keep your own eyes and ears open to these telltale signs. When you detect any of the signs, you can position yourself for more aggressive actions so that you can pinpoint the problem and follow up with appropriate action.

MEASURING CUSTOMER SATISFACTION ISN'T SO EASY

How do you compare the service you give customers with what they receive in a different market or other unrelated industry? The service ratings your customers give you and another company depend on their own or friends' experiences with the products of both companies. Your customers, however, still might have difficulty in making comparisons.

The problem is that customer service does not have a range of concrete measurements for different markets or unrelated industries. Customer service can be measured and agreed to by people only in the same field. However, a procedure of establishing concrete measurement standards has begun and is beginning to exert its influence within the industry where it was initiated. For example, your company may decide to promote a claim for fast service by providing part of the service free or paying $5 if the customer has to wait more than 10 minutes.

But there is little evidence proving that to be highly profitable, a company or organization must give superior customer service. If customers are equally dissatisfied with all companies, and if they are unable to compare the service offered in the field with that in other fields, the situation likely can continue.

Not-for-profit organizations also supply service, both good and bad. Most of these organizations determine their success in ways other than the amount of profit they make. Meeting contribution or membership goals is one of those ways.

Timing and evaluating short- versus long-term profits are factors. If a particular company's service levels decline and cause the company to lose its customers, quick cost-cutting or prompt acquiring of new customers can prevent the decline in service from affecting profitability. But when there are no further cost-reduction steps to take or any new customers in sight, the service decline eventually will hurt the company,

Last, there are some customer-service variables that simply resist measurement. For example, how do you measure your degree of empathy and the consequent attention you give a customer who is returning a purchase with the empathy and attention given by a competitor's employee in a similar situation? Until such variables are measurable or eliminated as factors, good or bad customer service will remain subjective.

QUICK TIPS

- **Be a counselor.** Ask customers what areas are troublesome. If your service isn't part of the solution, offer suggestions for improving the situation. Always act as a counselor to the customer.

- **Smile.** Words of wisdom from Dorothy Sayles, a customer service trainer in Chicago: "You probably should be in a different field if you haven't by now seen that you should be happy to see customers, that you should be happy to be of service. Without customers, you wouldn't have a job. So smile!"

- **Ask yourself: "Who'd miss me?"** Quality programs say you should please all customers — internal and external. But how do you identify them? "Ask yourself, 'If I stopped doing what I do for two weeks, who would complain?'" suggests Lisa Ford, founder of Ford & Associates training and consulting company. This test can help remind you just how important your job is.

- **Build morale.** Ask your employer to set up a "morale coupon" plan, *Communication Briefings* publisher Don Bagin suggests. When you see coworkers carrying out outstanding service with customers, give them a coupon. After they've earned five, they deserve a prize.

- **Handle calls personally.** Pleasantries such as "good morning" and "good afternoon" help convey a positive impression to customers. But you can take personalization a step further by identifying the customer as soon as possible. Use their names throughout the conversation to demonstrate that you are personally interested in them.

- **Meet top three expectations.** Quality revolves around three service characteristics, says research by American Express: timeliness, accuracy, and responsiveness. Type those three words on a card and keep them in view when you're serving customers. The reminder can help keep your efforts on track.

QUIZ

'PEOPLE SKILLS' ESSENTIAL TO QUALITY SERVICE

"I've been promoted to a job in which I'll be dealing with customers every day. I've been told that I'm very friendly and helpful, but is this enough? What special skills do I need to project a positive image of myself and my company?"

— S.A.A., Parkersburg, West Virginia

Dealing with customers is an important job because you represent your entire company with every interaction. The skills you will need to succeed fall into two categories: product/service knowledge and "people skills." A complete understanding of your company's products and services can be acquired by studying company literature and asking questions. People skills are somewhat less easily obtained. The following questions will help you determine what people skills you need.

1. Do you expect the best from people? _____

2. Can you remember other people's names? _____

3. When someone is talking, can you devote your full attention to what is being said? _____

4. Can you accept others' views, decisions, and behaviors, even if they are contrary to your own? _____

5. Are you lavish with praise and stingy with criticism? _____

6. Do you sincerely sympathize with others' troubles and take pleasure in their successes? _____

7. Do you look people directly in the eye? _____

8. Are you willing to admit your mistakes and correct them? _____

9. When talking to an angry or hostile person, can you avoid getting upset? _____

10. Do you make it a point never to get a cheap laugh at the expense of others? _____

YOUR PEOPLE PROSPECTS: If you had seven or more Yes responses, your people skills are in good shape. If you scored lower, remember that the kind of skills you need to work well with customers goes far beyond being polite and knowing when to smile. Customer service involves conflict resolution, negotiation, psychology, temper control, nonverbal interpretation, and, yes, a little mindreading. But don't let all that intimidate you. If you genuinely like people and are sincerely proud of the product or service your organization provides, you should find customer service very rewarding.

YOUR QUALITY TAKE-AWAY

Creating Quality Frontline Customer Service
What *You* Can Do

Quality processes often get their start on the factory floor, where the focus is on manufacturing standards and manufacturing consistency. But there is another aspect of quality that cannot be ignored: customer service. Because the ultimate goal of every business is customer satisfaction, pleasing customers has to be a major component of any quality effort. You, the front-line customer service rep, are the human link between the customer and all the behind-the-scenes quality actions and processes that take place in an organization.

- Acquire feedback from customers to help your organization deliver the quality customers expect.

- Provide courtesy service that is fast and efficient. Make customers feel important. Be responsive to their questions and to their needs.

- Develop techniques for relieving stress and for keeping your composure during difficult customer contacts.

- Build partnerships with customers. Always keep in mind that the customer indirectly pays your salary. Seeing customers who are happy and satisfied can be very rewarding.

The "people skills" you develop in customer service will help you be considered for promotion and can only advance your future career opportunities.

CHAPTER TEN

DELIVERING SUPER SUPPORT STAFF QUALITY

"A good secretary can save the boss more time in a year than a business jet can."

— MALCOLM BALDRIGE,
UNITED STATES SECRETARY OF COMMERCE (1981–1987)

INTRODUCTION

The traditional image of the secretary as a driving, yet somewhat invisible, force behind management is a thing of the past, according to a new survey. In fact, today, many secretaries perform functions of their former bosses. What these increasing responsibilities mean is that secretaries and other office support staff have a greater role than ever in advancing their organization's quality goals.

The survey of secretaries in the United States and Canada, conducted by the Administrative Development Institute, a company that provides training and information for office professionals, reveals that the corporate restructuring trend of the '90s has expanded the role of the secretary in management. Since 1990, 71 percent of the secretaries surveyed have gained a wide array of management duties, such as hiring, training, and supervising personnel — as well as supervising quality-management programs and purchasing office equipment.

Because corporate restructuring often results in the elimination or redefinition of management positions, secretaries have picked up duties formerly performed by middle managers. Companies that have changed to a team-oriented corporate structure frequently assign management to secretarial staffers.

How do secretaries feel about this trend? The survey shows that 55 percent of the secretaries surveyed say that corporate restructuring has had a positive impact on their jobs, as well as on their satisfaction with those jobs. Nearly 75 percent say that they are excited about their new responsibilities.

However, this redefinition of the secretary's role may be a mixed blessing. Only 53 percent of these secretaries have had training to help them perform their new responsibilities, and a small number have received training in areas directly related to their new duties. For example, although 43 percent of secretaries are responsible for personnel training, only half of them receive training in this area.

Office support staff aren't always visible to outside customers. But they are the lifeblood of a company's quality program. As their job role expands, every secretary should make a commitment to personal quality. Where training falls short, they should take the initiative to develop the new skills needed to meet their responsibilities.

One way to start is by asking yourself these questions:

- Do I take quality seriously?
- Am I clear about the quality goals of our team, or department, and our organization?
- Do I regularly assess how my actions meet those goals?
- Do I regard my coworkers as valued customers?
- Do I make full use of all our resources?
- Do I check the quality of my own work?
- Do I demand quality from my coworkers and from my organization?

Strive to answer those questions with a resounding "Yes." And for more ways to increase your personal quality in the office, review the following information.

SHOULD YOU COMPROMISE QUALITY FOR SPEED?

Out of concern for quality, you make sure everything is right before you consider it complete. But despite your efforts, your boss often complains that you take too much time, and that perfectionism holds up the rest of the department on its work. Should you forget about the quality of the work and just give him immediate results?

It's great to be conscientious about the quality of your work. Your boss probably appreciates it to a point, but there is a point at which you can go overboard and affect not only your productivity, but your boss's and the department's as well. Your boss is not asking you to forget about quality, but to keep your work balanced. Use the following tips to help you:

1. Determine what is important and what isn't. Your work time is limited, and you are probably under tight deadlines. Try to clearly define what your priorities are and how they match up with those of your department.

2. Outline a schedule. Write out your deadlines for each project, and then break down each one into steps. Estimate how long each step will take you in minutes, hours, or days. If your calculations take you beyond the set deadline, review your steps and see if any can be shortened or eliminated.

3. Determine how many times you need to double-check details. If you are checking and rechecking your work, you may be wasting valuable time.

4. Organize your work. If you don't take a systematic approach to work, you may mistakenly forget about something that you should have done and have to retrace your steps.

5. Increase your concentration. One of the reasons you feel the need to check and recheck your work may be because you are not concentrating enough. Try to tune out distractions and focus on what you are doing.

6. Write it down. If you have a hard time remaining on a specific schedule, at the start of each day write down what you need to accomplish. List priorities that must get done for the production process to flow smoothly. This will help keep you and your department on track.

10 WAYS TO STRENGTHEN QUALITY PERFORMANCE

Think about the way you interact at the office. Are you perceived as a professional? If coworkers know they can count on you, do they also see you as someone who works well with the entire team? Someone who takes on more responsibility than expected?

Here are 10 ways to strengthen your quality performance in the workplace. Implement them and you'll enjoy your job more — and attain greater success.

1. Be flexible. A world exists away from your work station; be open to learning tasks that don't directly relate to your job. Employers like staff members who can perform a range of duties. You'll not only impress others with your willingness to comply — you'll also learn and grow.

2. Sharpen your grammar and writing skills. Above average oral communication skills are important in your contact by telephone. But much modern technology — including e-mail and fax machines — puts a premium on the ability to communicate in writing.

3. Be congenial. Success on the job involves treating everyone in a friendly and professional manner. Everyone enjoys their day more when they work in a pleasant atmosphere.

4. Keep phone skills up to date. Are there helpful features on the phone that you still don't use? Stretch your productivity by knowing everything about your phone system.

5. Know how to use office equipment. Don't stop with the phone system. Make yourself indispensable by knowing what to do when a computer, copier, or fax machine malfunctions.

6. Study your industry. Know where your company fits in. Become familiar with the competition, too, and with related fields.

7. Think critically. To thrive in the workplace, show that you can analyze problems, prioritize tasks, take the initiative, and solve any customer problem that comes your way.

8. Look great! If workers look bad, a company looks bad. Even if you aren't seen by outside customers, always look your best. Even on "casual" days, don't be caught off guard.

9. Take classes, inside and outside your field. Take advantage of opportunities to learn on the job. But don't stop learning at the end of the day. Pursue night classes. You may love your job, but don't let that make you complacent about exploring the world outside. Knowledge increases your value to your company and your options within your career.

10. Be businesslike. To be taken seriously and treated with respect, carry on in a businesslike manner. Give your best effort — and let others know that you stand by your actions.

SKILLS ASSESSMENT CAN BOOST PERFORMANCE

Under the fierce pressure and fast pace of our day-to-day routines, it's easy to lose sight of the skills on which we draw constantly in our jobs. And yet, it can be a valuable exercise to identify the unique strengths that fuel our daily efforts. "The process can make your work more rewarding and help you develop skills that will enhance your performance and further your career," observes Ethel Cook, president of Corporate Improvement Group.

Here's how Cook recommends that you identify and build your professional skills:

1. Assess the skills needed for your job. Make a list of the skills needed by office professionals. Then, be as objective as possible in rating yourself as "good," "average," or "weak" in each category. Your list might include word processing, filing, writing reports and/or memos, organizational skills, listening ability, as well as many other skills more specific to your company or industry.

2. Acknowledge your professional skills. Compile a list of verbs to help you identify the skills you use in your daily tasks. Some examples might be: administer, budget, catalog, coordinate, edit, implement, organize, prioritize, schedule, and train. You should be able to add verbs to this list. Just visualize what you do in a day, in a week, and so on. Then, compile a list of projects you are working on or have worked on recently. Finally, select three of these projects to explore in detail. For each, list the tasks you performed to accomplish the project. Drawing on your list of verbs, note the skills you used to perform each task.

3. Share what you've learned about your skills. "Whenever the opportunity arises, let people know about the skills you're using on the job," advises Cook. "For example, when colleagues ask how or what you're doing, tell them, using your skill verbs: 'I've been coordinating the marketing services for our upcoming trade show.' This will influence their perception of you as a highly skilled, action-oriented professional," she notes.

4. Develop a skills enhancement plan. First, identify the professional skills that are important to you in your career. Ask yourself, "What skills will I need to develop in the coming year? In the next five years?" Look at business trends for clues. For example, learning to operate on the Internet would be a smart goal for the coming year.

Write an action plan for developing the skills you will need. Include taking courses that will help you grow, exploring new software, and undertaking research on technological advances affecting office work.

WHEN YOU'VE BEEN PASSED OVER FOR A PROMOTION

You wanted that promotion so much you could taste it. You paid your dues, talked to the right people, and took the appropriate night-school courses. In short, you did all the right things to prepare you for a new position. Despite all your efforts, the promotion you thought was in the bag went to someone else. You're stunned, angry, and greatly disappointed. You consider marching into your boss's office and resigning on the spot.

Being passed over for a promotion is one of the toughest disappointments to face in a career. Anger, bitterness, frustration, and downright hostility are common and understandable reactions in a situation like this. But the way you handle your reaction can have a significant impact on your chances for advancement when the next promotion opportunity arises. Losing out on a promotion is a permanent setback only if you allow it to be.

Here are some ideas for managing your reaction in this difficult situation:

- Share your feelings of disappointment and anger with someone outside the organization. Resist the temptation to cry on the shoulder of sympathetic coworkers. While it may momentarily make you feel better, you may be recruited by some for routine company-bashing sessions. Don't say anything to a coworker that you wouldn't want to reach the boss's ear.

- Discuss your experience, skills, and abilities with your manager or a trusted senior member of your organization who is familiar with your work. Ask this person the following questions: What should I do more (or less) of? What should I keep doing? The answers to these questions may help you gain greater insight into areas needing development that you were unaware of.

- Talk to the person who made the hiring decision. It is absolutely essential to wait until you have cooled down from your initial disappointment before doing this. In a calm, nonconfrontational matter, ask which skills and qualities you lacked for the job. Don't ask, "Why was John Smith hired instead of me?" Rather, ask, "Can you tell me about the factors the final decision was based on?"

  Don't put the other person in the position of having to defend the decision. Remember that you are seeking information, not justification. Ask what you might do differently or what specific skills you need to have a better shot next time.

- Don't resign within the next few weeks, no matter how tempting it might be. The gratification you'd feel is fleeting at best. Eventually, you're the one to lose out. Others will assume it's sour grapes on your part, which may not help the quality of future reference checks. That doesn't mean that you should pass up any good opportunities that come along. Just make it clear that you're not leaving out of spite.

- Be gracious to the person who got the job, no matter how hard it is. It's vital that you treat this person with the same respect you'd demand. Ultimately, you will only hurt your own reputation by speaking ill of the promoted coworker or undermining his or her efforts. This is a time when you must swallow that pride and be gracious.

It's also important to realize there may have been factors beyond your control that influenced the final decision. As difficult as this time is, the hurt will pass. If you use the situation as an opportunity to learn more about yourself, others will likely be impressed with your ability to handle the situation with an incomparably professional style. Chances are when the next promotion comes around, your maturity and commitment will be remembered. The next time you go for the brass ring, your chances of grasping it will be that much greater!

A Credo to Live By

Whenever you find your spirits flagging, review these tenets to live by:

- **Believe in yourself completely.** Have faith in your ability to do anything you set your mind to.

- **Believe in what you are doing.** Know that you have the ability to help others find solutions to their problems.

- **See yourself as successful.** Virtually everyone has some redeeming qualities. Develop a self-image that includes personal success.

- **Appreciate your assets.** Demonstrate in appearance, manner, voice, and spirit that you have value to your company.

- **Recognize the importance and value of others.** Strive to enhance the quality of life for everyone you touch; remember, they ultimately contribute to your own quality of life.

- **Like yourself.** The more you like yourself, the more generous you'll be toward others.

- **Look on your problems as opportunities.** Welcome change and the challenges you face. They give you a chance to stretch your abilities.

- **Plan your work well, then work your plan.** Live by your own agenda. When flying through each day, sit in the pilot's seat instead of in the passenger section.

- **Allow yourself the luxury of enthusiasm.** It can make or break even the best-laid plans.

ADD 'MASTER JUGGLER' TO JOB DESCRIPTION

What's the most important skill an administrative assistant can have today?

Juggling.

You'll need that skill judging by a recent survey, which says that today's secretary supports an average of four professionals. That means four schedules, four sets of job tasks, four sets of expectations. Too bad it doesn't mean four extra hands for the assistant! The survey was developed by OfficeTeam, a national staffing service, and conducted by an independent research firm. Approximately 150 managers and human resource executives from some of the nation's 1,000 largest companies were surveyed. "Technology has made administrative assistants much more efficient in their jobs and the increased productivity is enabling them to support more managers and take on more varied duties," says Andrew Denka, executive director of OfficeTeam.

Executives are doing their part with the help of computer software programs. In a related survey, for example, managers said they now type almost half (47 percent) of their own business correspondence. "Word processing software, with its editing and cut-and-paste features, has simplified the creation of letters and other documents," notes Denka. "Managers have become more accustomed to composing as they type, thus streamlining the process."

So if you report to multiple people and have to juggle all their needs and requirements, you're in good company.

CLEAR THE MIND (AND DESK DRAWERS)

With its multitude of desk drawers, filing cabinets, and other nooks and crannies, the modern office and workplace is often used as much as a place storeroom as a place for getting things done.

How about setting aside an afternoon for a general cleanup of your entire work area? Periodic cleanups can work wonders when trying to unclog offices. Clearing the decks can help give your team a psychological lift, a fresh start, as it embarks on its quality improvement effort.

Keep in mind these tips before launching an office cleanup day:

- First clear the effort with the boss. Perhaps she can sanction it as an official casual day so workers don't have to worry about messing up their good work clothes.

- Select the time carefully, picking a normally quiet day or season.

- Involve the whole department. (Some businesses have annual company-wide cleanup days.)

- Create a fun atmosphere by providing soft drinks and other refreshments.

- Have enough refuse containers on hand.

- Recycle whatever you can — white paper, newsprint, and aluminum cans.

- Make sure staffers are still able to answer phone calls or conduct routine business.

- Adopt the mindset that you're willing to throw away unnecessary materials.

- Establish a table or other area for those unnecessary or unwanted objects and materials that are just "too good" to throw away. Let coworkers look over the "merchandise" to see if they can use any of it — preferably at home.

COURTESY AT THE PHOTO COPIER

You may take for granted a basic element of functioning as a team on a daily basis — learning to share resources, including office equipment. Sharing equipment, including copiers, fax machines, and computers and their printers, can be inconvenient. But observing a few basic rules of courtesy can minimize the problems for everyone, says Barbara Pachter, coauthor of *The Complete Guide to Business Etiquette* (Irwin Professional Publishing).

When sharing a copier or printer, her tips are:

- **Take care of essential maintenance.** Replace toner or clear paper jams when necessary. When you're done, replenish the paper supply. Be sure to return machines to their original settings (most likely one copy, 8 $\frac{1}{2}$" x 11") for the next person.

- **Observe protocol for large jobs.** If you're making a large number of copies, be gracious about interruptions. If someone comes along to make two or three copies, let him or her in. Turnabout is fair play; so, if a coworker has a large copying project underway, you are within your rights to say, "Can I interrupt for a minute?" Also, if you know you'll be tying up the printer with a long document, alert other computer users.

- **Respect the need for confidentiality.** If teammates leave papers behind at the copier or have yet to pick them up from the printer, either put them aside — face down — or return them.

When sharing access to a computer:

- **Honor schedules.** Be cooperative about coordinating and scheduling projects, so each user knows exactly when he or she can access the equipment. But, also know when to be flexible and give precedence to a peer with a top-priority task.

- **Assess your computer time carefully.** Unless you're realistic about how long it will take you to complete a computer task, you could end up going over your allotted time. Then, you risk interfering with everyone else's schedules and, ultimately, throwing the whole department off.

- **Call a troubleshooter or repairperson immediately when problems arise.** Never just walk away and leave the problem to someone else. If everyone did that, it would never get done.

- **Don't arbitrarily change any programming.** Always check with whoever is in charge of your team's computer before making any changes. And then, make sure you know what you're doing.

- **Ask permission** before using teammates' disks, files, or passwords. These are their personal property and deserve respect.

These rules can apply to sharing almost any piece of office

equipment. Have respect for your teammates' need to use these resources, and they will return the favor.

THE 1, 2, 3's OF GETTING ALONG

Are you often frustrated at how difficult it is to get along with others? You can make it easier by following these 10 basic rules established by Norman Vincent Peale.

1. Remember people's names.

2. Be a comfortable (not stressful) person to be with.

3. Lighten up. Don't let every little thing get you down.

4. Give humility a chance. Don't be a know-it-all.

5. Be an interesting person to know. Work to cultivate a variety of interests so that others will find your company intellectually stimulating.

6. Stop behaviors that obviously annoy other people.

7. Offer your support to those who need it.

8. Make an effort to like people. Eventually, it'll come naturally.

9. Try to clear up misunderstandings and deal with grievances that drain your energy.

10. Clarify your values and beliefs, and develop spiritual depth. Use your inner strength to help others.

THE PROS KNOW: TIPS FROM READERS

• **Colored warning keeps fax in business.** "The fax machine in our office is running constantly, either sending or receiving documents. Often the paper would run out, and we wouldn't be able to receive faxes. Now we put a piece of colored paper toward the bottom of the stack in the paper tray. This alerts us to the fact that the paper is getting low before it's too late."

— CINDY SVOBODA,
SCOTTSBLUFF, NEBRASKA

• **Communication doesn't stop with top boss.** "The secret to being a great team is communication. As a division secretary, I receive correspondence for information and/or necessary action to be taken. I forward it to the responsible branch managers and their secretaries (to let the right hand know what the left hand is doing). This allows the secretary to take action, in case the boss is out or too busy to address the issue. Thus, deadlines are always met on time."

— MARY ANN HERNANDEZ,
AUSTIN, TEXAS

• **Plain labels save money, time.** "Today, when we need to be careful about wasting our office supplies, I have come up with a solution that cuts down on expenses as well as saves time. When we need to mail out something, we type the addresses on small, plain 1" x 3" dot matrix labels. We then attach these to the more expensive labels and envelopes with the company logo. If we make a mistake typing the label, it's much more economical to throw away a plain label than to throw away the more expensive items. It also saves time when you need to type a number of envelopes. Just stick a sheet of labels in the typewriter, and you don't have to keep inserting each envelope as you type."

— SUSAN PLEGGE,
LITTLE ROCK, ARKANSAS

• **Log shows boss need for project warning.** "Our new division head came from a much smaller company and had difficulty grasping how many tasks our staff handles. His habit was to wait until he had a new project ready to hand off to us before letting us know of its existence. This could put us in a real time crunch. After this happened two or three times, I started keeping a log on my desk calendar of my daily jobs. I take a few minutes on Monday to type the list of jobs done the previous week. This list was the tool the boss needed to see the impact his untimely projects had on the staff. He now gives us advance notice so we can anticipate and plan for special projects."

— SALLY SPARKMAN,
SANTA MONICA, CALIFORNIA

• **Voice mail jogs boss' memory.** "At the end of each day, I leave my boss a message on voice mail or on his answering machine at home with his appointments for the next day, including any pertinent information. Then, if he forgets his calendar or needs any information, all he has to do is check his messages in the morning."

— PAT MAZZA,
SCHAUMBURG, ILLINOIS

Quick Tips

- **Tell it like it is.** If the boss asks you to handle a task that will cause the rest of your workload to be disrupted, explain the situation. Say you will be happy to do the job, but it will have the following effects. Then, let the boss decide if his or her task is critical enough to displace your other jobs.

- **Leave no phone unanswered.** Establish backup procedures so no phone rings more than two or three times in your area before it is answered. If everyone is tied up in a meeting, be sure all have activated their voice-mail or made arrangements so callers can leave messages.

- **Plan your mornings.** The first hour of the workday is when people are most alert, reports *Working Smart*, a National Institute of Business publication. Take advantage of this high-energy time by planning problem-solving and brainstorming sessions bright and early. Before you leave work for the day, plan how you will best utilize this time the following morning.

- **Make time for mundane tasks.** Set aside a few hours a week to go through your in-box. Friday afternoon is often a good time to tackle this mundane task. Letting items pile up makes it easier to overlook issues that need to be addressed. Work it into your weekly schedule so that it becomes routine.

- **Write your quality book.** To maintain the level of quality established in your department, create a "quality handbook" for temporary employees or anyone filling in for you. List your job functions, personal work mottoes, priorities, and tips.

- **Remember, small courtesies count.** Remember that office equipment, such as copiers and staplers, don't restock themselves. If you use something up, take a second to replenish the supply. Everyone else's time is valuable, just as yours is.

- **Flash card reminder.** "Good morning, I mean, afternoon. Can I help you?" Does that sound like you, stumbling over your a.m./p.m. phone greeting? Simple solution: Make up a bright neon card with "Good morning" printed on one side and "Good afternoon" printed on the other. Place the card above your phone as a quick reminder. Now if you can just remember to flip the card over at noon!

DO YOU HAVE A CLEAR CAREER PLAN?

"My supervisor recently praised my performance and said I will go a long way in my career as a secretary. I appreciated her comments. But what she doesn't know is that I see this position as just one link in my career path. I envision myself someday in a position that ranks higher on the company flow chart. What can I do to be sure I have what it takes to keep growing?"

— W.H., Dallas, Texas

Most people have a desire to get ahead in their careers. But it takes resolve to realize that ambition. You probably have plenty of competition out there. So, the trick is to stand out from the crowd and be recognized as uniquely qualified. This quiz might help you determine how to set out. Answer each question Yes or No and score yourself.

1. Do you set specific high-level, yet achievable, goals for yourself? _____

2. Do you continually evaluate your performance and behavior with these goals in mind? _____

3. Do you aggressively and regularly seek to upgrade your skills and knowledge? _____

4. Do you pinpoint high achievers as role models from whom you can learn? _____

5. Are you ready and willing to make sacrifices to reach your goals? _____

6. Do you compare your performance with others who compete with you for recognition and status? _____

7. Do you go out of your way to help your boss meet his or her professional objectives? _____

8. Are you loyal to your company? _____

9. Do you seek feedback on how to do your job better or expand your areas of responsibility? _____

10. Though competitive, do you have a high ethical standard in the way you treat others? _____

YOUR CAREER PLAN SCORE: A score of eight or more Yes answers ranks you above the crowd in career planning. Chances are that management notices your high performance. A score of six or seven is fair. You may want to reevaluate your career strategies. A lower score suggests that you are destined to stay where you are professionally. Take corrective measures now!

YOUR QUALITY TAKE-AWAY

Delivering Super Support Staff Quality
What *You* Can Do

Due to downsizing, reengineering, and other changes, secretaries and other support staff personnel carry out more responsibilities in the workplace than ever before. That means if you are an office professional today, you have an increasing role in advancing your company's quality initiatives — improving human relations, strengthening communication, building team spirit, and meeting customers' expectations. It also places you in an excellent position for greater career growth possibilities.

- Be sure you understand your organization's quality goals and participate visibly in the quality development process.

- Take advantage of workshops and other training that is available to you.

- Strengthen your interpersonal skills, keep up with evolving technology, and maintain a professional and businesslike appearance.

- Look for ways to prevent mistakes.

- Think of the next person in the work process as your valued customer. Do your best to get along with others in your office. Remember, personal quality involves meeting both other people's and your own demands and expectations.

Secretaries and office support personnel almost always know how to use the latest computer program or new equipment long before the boss knows; in fact, the boss usually learns them from the secretary! In the ever-evolving workplace, flexibility is a valuable asset. It will serve you well in your current position and throughout your career.

QUALITY 1ST

It's an old-fashioned idea that's going to take business into the 21st century. QUALITY is the watchword in today's business environment — consumers demand quality first; that's why your employees need Dartnell's **Quality 1st** newsletter program. The main goal of this biweekly periodical is to help you create quality-minded employees. Each installment instills and reinforces an unshakable commitment to quality products and services, and dedication to excellence in one's own work. **Quality 1st** will help your employees understand that top-quality work can lead to greater job satisfaction, job security and greater advancement.
Order # 5008

Yes, send me the book(s) or newsletter I have checked. I understand that if I am not completely satisfied, I may return the book(s) or newsletter within 30 days for a full refund.

_____**TELEPHONE TERRIFIC!**; $10.95
    Book code: 8492

_____**QUALITY 1ST NEWSLETTER**
(Minimum order 5 copies, shipped biweekly)
Order # 5008
5 to 9 copies.....................$1.59 each
10 to 49 copies...................$1.49 each
50 to 99 copies...................$1.45 each
100 to 249 copies................$1.40 each
        (Payable annually)

_____**STANDOUT SERVICE**; $13.95
    Book code: 8123

_____**TOUGH CUSTOMERS**; $13.95
    Book Code: 8124

_____**THE EXTRA MILE**; $13.95
    Book Code: 8122

BILL MY: ❏ VISA   ❏ AMERICAN EXPRESS   ❏ MASTERCARD   ❏ COMPANY

CARD NUMBER _____ EXP. DATE _____

NAME_____ TITLE _____

COMPANY _____

ADDRESS _____

CITY/STATE/ZIP _____

SIGNATURE _____ PHONE_____
        (Signature and phone number are necessary to process order.)   96-5506

❏ Please send me your latest catalog

Copies may be ordered from your bookseller or from Dartnell.
To order from Dartnell, call toll free **(800) 621-5463**
or fax us your order **(800) 327-8635**

DARTNELL

4660 N RAVENSWOOD AVE, CHICAGO, IL 60640-4595 PHONE: (800) 621-5463 or FAX: (800) 327-86